D1589182

THE LION AND THE TIGER

Denis Judd is Professor of British Imperial, Commonwealth, and Indian History at the London Metropolitan University. He is the author of numerous books, including the best-selling *Empire: the British Imperial Experience from 1865 to the Present* (Phoenix Press, 2001) and, most recently, *The Boer War* (John Murray, 2003). He has written radio documentaries for BBC Radio 4 and the World Service, and has broadcast many times as a presenter, consultant, and major interviewee for television and radio programmes, most recently for BBC TV Newsnight, BBC Radio 3 Nightwaves, Channel 4, ITV, South African TV, and for BBC Radio 4's 'Vestiges – the British Empire'.

THE LION AND THE TIGER

The Rise and Fall of the British Raj,

1600–1947

DENIS JUDD

OXFORD
UNIVERSITY PRESS

OXFORD
UNIVERSITY PRESS

Great Clarendon Street, Oxford OX2 6DP

Oxford University Press is a department of the University of Oxford.
It furthers the University's objective of excellence in research, scholarship,
and education by publishing worldwide in

Oxford New York

Auckland Cape Town Dar es Salaam Hong Kong Karachi
Kuala Lumpur Madrid Melbourne Mexico City Nairobi
New Delhi Shanghai Taipei Toronto

With offices in

Argentina Austria Brazil Czech Republic France Greece
Guatemala Hungary Italy Japan South Korea Poland Portugal
Singapore Switzerland Thailand Turkey Ukraine Vietnam

Published in the United States
by Oxford University Press Inc., New York

© Denis Judd

The moral rights of the author has been asserted
Database right Oxford University Press (maker)

First published 2004

First published as an Oxford University Press Paperback 2005

All rights reserved. No part of this publication may be reproduced,
stored in a retrieval system, or transmitted, in any form or by any means,
without the prior permission in writing of Oxford University Press,
or as expressly permitted by law, or under terms agreed with the appropriate
reprographics rights organization. Enquiries concerning reproduction
outside the scope of the above should be sent to the Rights Department,
Oxford University Press, at the address above

You must not circulate this book in any other binding or cover
and you must impose this same condition on any acquirer

British Library Cataloguing in Publication Data

Data available

Library of Congress Cataloging in Publication Data

Data available

ISBN 0-19-280579-7

I

Typeset by Footnote Graphics Limited, Warminster, Wiltshire
Printed in Great Britain
on acid-free paper by
Clays Ltd, St Ives plc

To Sam,
may you go from strength to strength

Preface

The author would like to thank a number of people who have been vital to the writing and publication of this book. Thanks first of all to Katharine Reeve for commissioning the book, and for her enthusiastic support throughout. Thanks also to Emily Jolliffe for her friendly editorial help, and to Hilary Walford for her extraordinarily meticulous copy-editing. Sarah Kidd and Kate Farquhar-Thomson have been wonderful publicists. The London Metropolitan University provided generous research relief. Without the intelligent, good-humoured, and efficient assistance of Meryl Wilson it is doubtful whether the book would have got to press on time and in so good a shape. Finally, I would like to dedicate this book to my oldest grandson, Sam, aged 7, who has had so much to cope with over the last few years, but who has maintained throughout not only his courage but also his passionate interest in books. I hope that one day this book will be enjoyed by him.

Denis Judd
London, 2004

Contents

CONTENTS

List of Plates

I

'To fly to India for gold': Early Contacts, 1583–1615

The British experience with India began in earnest over 400 years ago, during the reign of Queen Elizabeth I, when a few merchants humbly applied for trading concessions from the apparently all-powerful Mughal emperor. For many years, the English interlopers and traders who made contact with the sub-continent were viewed by Indian observers, especially by the various power elites, as little more than pirates and potentially troublesome, conquering barbarians.

From these inauspicious and simple beginnings, however, the British became the undisputed masters of a vast and densely populated subcontinent. Indeed, Britain's possession of India, triumphantly confirmed by the beginning of the nineteenth century, seemed to demonstrate more than anything else its towering imperial, naval, and commercial status as the world's first super power. From the British point of view, Empire without India was unthinkable. The cliché describing India as 'the jewel in the Crown' was no hyperbole, but a precise and vividly accurate definition of India's importance to Britain's imperial experience and prosperity. When British rule eventually ended in 1947, 80 per cent of the Empire's subjects gained their independence at one stroke.

Interestingly, the first mention of an Englishman setting foot in India is over 1,000 years earlier, and can be found in the *Anglo-Saxon Chronicle*, one of the earliest records of the history of the English. According to this source, King Alfred the Great sent a certain Sighelm on a pilgrimage to India in AD 883. Sighelm apparently brought back 'many strange and precious unions [pearls] and costly spices'.[1] Although there seems to have been no significant follow-up to this remarkable initiative of Sighelm and Alfred the Great, the commercial lure of India, and of the trade that crossed its frontiers and left its ports, was increasingly known and increasingly attractive to Europeans.

During the late Middle Ages, however, almost all the spices and exotic goods that poured through India and the Indian Ocean into the insatiable markets of Europe reached the Mediterranean through the prosperous ports of the Levant. European merchants thus had to rely upon middlemen for the supply of commodities that were both desirable and highly profitable. Given the complexities of the relationship of Western Europe with the eastern Mediterranean and the chronic conflict between an expansionist Islam and Christianity, not to speak of the bitter legacy of the crusades to the Holy Land, it was only a matter of time before Europeans sought direct and more profitable contact with the Indian market.

Driven by the power of these market forces, by the end of the fifteenth century two European explorers claimed to have found other sea routes to the Indies. Christopher Columbus, who had crossed the Atlantic in 1492, went to his deathbed still convinced that he had discovered the East Indies rather than the West Indies. More realistically, Vasco da Gama, sailing for Portugal in 1497, actually did round the southern tip of Africa, and went on to reach the spice port of Calicut on the Malabar coast of south-western India in 1498.

This was a landing of the utmost significance in the relationship between Europe and India. Da Gama's epic voyage fired the imagination, and the commercial hopes, of Europeans throughout the continent. The English, who in 1497 had sent Sebastian and John Cabot to discover Newfoundland, shared the excitement. Under the Tudors, England, though still heavily reliant on its trade with Europe, and still possessing Calais as its foothold there, was turning out to the wider world. Soon English trade would be flowing not merely to the Indies, both East and West, but also to North America and beyond.

Under the dynamic and self-confident rule of the archetypal Renaissance prince, Henry VIII (king from 1509 to 1547), voices were raised demanding that the English staked their claim to the profits of trade with India. 'The Indies are discovered', proclaimed a petition sent to the young King Henry VIII in 1511, 'and vast treasure brought from thence every day. Let us therefore bend our endeavours thitherwards; and if the Spaniards and the Portuguese suffer us not to join with them, there will be yet region enough for all to enjoy.'[2]

The allure and exotic mystery of India intrigued English writers and scholars. English poets enriched their work with references to India and the East. Christopher Marlowe, the Elizabethan playwright, wrote:

> Men from the farthest equinoctial line
> Have swarmed in troops into the Eastern India,
> Lading their ships with gold and precious stones,
> And made their spoils . . .[3]

Marlowe returned to this theme in *Faustus*: 'Shall I make spirits fetch me what I please. . . . I'll have them fly to India for gold, Ransack the ocean for orient pearl, And search all corners of the new-found world For pleasant fruits and princely delicates [spices].'[4] Later, John Milton wrote in *Paradise Lost* of 'Agra and Lahor of Great Mogul'.[5]

4

Apart from finding literary inspiration, the English, though less ruthless and fanatical than the Spanish in their determination to Christianize and 'civilize' newly discovered territories, were increasingly anxious to export aspects of their own culture. The process was, however, by no means a one-sided experience. For example, in 1579 an English Jesuit, Thomas Stevens, went to India as Rector of the Jesuit College at Goa, and wrote letters to his father that were widely circulated. Father Stevens showed, however, that not only was India rich in trading possibilities, but that it contained cultural riches as well. He vividly described the Marathi language, which was widely spoken in west central India: 'Like a jewel among pebbles, like a sapphire among jewels, is the excellence of the Marathi tongue. Like the jasmine among blossoms, the musk among perfumes, the peacock among birds, the Zodiac among the stars, is Marathi among languages.'[6] These were hardly the sentiments of a blinkered cultural imperialist.

Trade, however, was a more down-to-earth activity. In 1583 a group of London merchants organized an expedition to India. Ralph Fitch, William Leeds, and James Story set sail in the *Tyger*. After landing at Tripoli in Syria, they followed the hazardous, barely imaginable, 3,000-mile-long overland route to India. Later, Fitch almost ecstatically sang the praises of what he had seen: 'Here is great traffic for all sorts of spices and drugs, silk and cloth of silk, elephants teeth and much China work, and much sugar which is made of the nut called "Gajara"; the tree is called the palmer: which is the profitablest tree in the world.'[7]

In 1600 a momentous step in the history of English relations with India took place. In December of that year, Queen Elizabeth I granted a charter to the 'Governor and Company of Merchants of London trading into the East Indies'. Under pressure from ambitious and lobbying English merchants, and shrewdly hoping for badly needed income from vast customs dues deriving from direct trade with the East, the Queen took an initiative that was to have unimaginable consequences. It was this company that was in due course to rise to paramount power in the sub-continent and to lay the foundations for the magnificent imperial structure of the British Raj.

Interestingly, the chief commercial hopes of the new company were not initially focused upon India. Instead, merchants hoped to break into the rich trade of the East Indian spice islands. For a whole variety of reasons, spices were clearly the trading commodity to secure. Much of Europe's livestock had to be slaughtered before each winter, which meant that spices were needed to preserve meat during the cold season. Spices also flavoured food in numerous exciting and satisfying ways. They also disguised the taste of meat that was either bad or becoming so.

The difficulty was that spice islands (small islands like Amboyna, Ternate, and Tidore, as well as the large East

Indian islands of Java, Sumatra, and the Celebes) already traded busily with the Dutch. It was, therefore, unlikely that the English East India Company would find it easy to break into the market, despite the fact that Elizabethan England had given important diplomatic and military support to its fellow Protestants in the Netherlands in their efforts to shake off Spanish rule.

Nonetheless, preparations were made for the first, crucial voyage. Among the early subscribers to the East India Company were these men: Nicholas Barnsley, Grocer, subscription £150; Henry Bridgman, Leatherseller, £200; James Deane, Draper, £300; Thomas Farrington, Vintner, £200; Leonard Halliday, Alderman, £1,000; Ralph Hamer, Merchant Tailor, £200; Sir Stephen Seame, Lord Mayor of London, £200; Thomas Smithe, Haberdasher, £200; Sir Richard Saltonstall and his children, £200; Richard Wiseman, Goldsmith, £200.

Under the command of James Lancaster, five vessels set sail on 13 February 1601. Among the goods they carried were '40 muskets; 18 swords; a pair of bellows; a standing bed with pillows . . . and curtains; 3 old brass ladles; 26 sponges'.[8] A year and a half later the expedition reached northern Sumatra. Perhaps unexpectedly, the local ruler welcomed them as representatives of the island power that had defeated the Spanish Armada in 1588. He also granted them freedom to trade, and proceeded to question them. One of the Englishmen left an interesting account of this:

> The King asked our General if our Queen were married, and how long she reigned, which when the General had answered by his interpreter, the King wondered. The King likewise told the General, if the words in her Majesty's letter came from the heart, he had cause to think well thereof. Dinner being ended, the King caused his Damsels to dance, and his women to play Music unto them, who were richly adorned with Bracelets and Jewels, and this was a great favour: for he does not usually let them be seen to any.[9]

Almost certainly, the Sumatrans had no use for many of the goods brought by the English—woollen vests and Devon trousers, for example—but this first contact of the East India Company with the East Indies had been friendly enough and promised a good deal. In good buccaneering tradition, James Lancaster added immediate profit to diplomatic goodwill when he plundered a laden Portuguese galleon in the Indies before sailing for England.

The English East India Company coexisted uneasily with the Dutch East India Company in the Indies between 1601 and 1623. Local conditions at first continued to favour them, as most indigenous people hated the Portuguese for their heavy handedness and their Christianizing Catholic zeal, and were glad to see them ousted by either of the two Protestant powers. The Dutch, however, were increasingly jealous of English activities and sought to stifle them.

The directors of the English East India Company were well aware of this:

If the present misunderstandings between the two nations should ferment to an open war, it would be thought by the vulgar but a war for pepper which they think to be [a] slight thing, because each family spends but a little [on] it. But at the bottom it will prove a war for the Dominion of the British as well as the Indian seas, because if ever they come to be sole masters of that Commodity, as they already are of nutmegs, mace, cloves, and cinnamon, the sole profit of that one commodity, pepper, being of general use, will be more to them than all the rest and in probability sufficient to defray the constant charge of a great navy in Europe.[10]

In 1623 there was a disaster for the English attempt to break into the commerce of the spice islands. This was what became known in English circles as the 'Massacre of Amboyna'. It was an incident that finally snuffed out the hopes of the English in the East Indies. Nineteen Englishmen were arrested on a trumped-up charge of conspiracy by the Dutch Governor of Amboyna, Van Speult. Confessions were tortured out of the unfortunate captives, ten of whom were eventually executed.

The violent and outraged reaction that these events provoked in England did not lead to any local response, though the propaganda war that ensued did much to sully the image of Dutch colonialism in English folk memory and perceptions. Although it took some time to take effect, time was up for the English East India Company in the region. By 1682 the last English factory, or trading centre, in the spice islands had been abandoned.

Ignominiously expelled from the East Indies, the English now concentrated on India as a second-best alternative. It was fortunate that the East India Company had made a landing on Indian soil in 1608. In that year William Hawkins arrived at Surat, a booming port on the west coast of India. The Portuguese were already established at Surat and naturally did not welcome Hawkins. As he was to write, he 'could not peep out of doors for fear of the Portugals, who in troops lay lurking in the by-ways to give me assault to murder me'. Nor did the Portuguese think much of Hawkins's letter of introduction from King James I. As Hawkins complained, they 'most vilely abused his Majesty, terming him King of fishermen and of an island of no importance'.[11]

Ambitious and determined, Hawkins at last set off, accompanied by a hired retinue, for Agra, the capital of the Mughal Emperor Jahangir (1605–28). This expedition clearly shows the humble beginnings of the English in India. In effect, Hawkins was just a lowly ambassador from a far away and virtually unknown island in a subcontinent where great civilizations had once flourished, and which, though it teemed with millions of people, and with conflicting religions and cultures, could still overawe and discomfort foreign visitors.

The Mughal Empire in India had been founded by Babur in the early sixteenth century. Babur had been born in a small principality in Central Asia, and had spent his

formative years in the commercially significant and cultur-
ally rich city of Samarkand. On his father's side he was
descended from Tamerlane, the destroyer of Delhi, and on
his mother's side from the Mongol warlord Genghis Khan—
hence the western term Mogul to describe the Mughals.

Establishing a base in Afghanistan, Babur invaded
India in 1517 and by 1529 had made himself master of an
empire stretching from the frontiers of Afghanistan to the
borders of Bengal. He spoke Persian, practised the faith of
Islam, and, despite his reputation for cold-blooded conquest, was also seen as a chivalrous, refined, and cultured
man. Followed by a glittering number of successors, men
like Humayun, Akbar, and Jahangir, by the time the
English tried to establish themselves on the subcontinent
the Mughals ruled, either directly or indirectly, over a vast
number of subject Indian territories.

For the moment Mughal suzerainty was effective,
though its supremacy was soon to decay and vanish.
Although the Mughals were Muslims, 70 per cent of the
Indian people were followers of the Hindu religion. Less
than 10 per cent (like Buddhists, Sikhs, or Parsees) avowed
other faiths. Thus, with only 20 per cent of the Indian
people belonging to Islam, the Mughal emperors exercised
a tactful sway in religious matters. On the other hand, the
complexity and diversity of Indian society meant that
determined interlopers like the English could attempt to
play off one sect or region against another.

The Emperor Jahangir welcomed Hawkins to his magnificent court, where the architecture, the culture, and the display made its equivalent in England seem down at heel and provincial. Jahangir was impressed by the Englishman's ability to speak Persian and also by his drinking capacity! He made Hawkins a senior member of his staff and even found him a Christian Armenian girl for a wife. Barely able to believe his luck, Hawkins wrote to the East India Company that he hoped all this would 'feather my nest and do you service'. The Company, however, got little out of his mission. The truth was that Jahangir was prudently weighing his diplomatic options, and concluded that it would be unwise to favour the English at the expense of the powerful and aggressive Portuguese.

In 1612, however, an English sea victory over the Portuguese, off Surat, finally persuaded Jahangir to grant the East India Company Surat as a factory. In practice, this meant little more than the right to trade. The Portuguese were still dangerous rivals, and the favours of the Emperor could be withdrawn at any moment.

In 1615, therefore, the East India Company sent Sir Thomas Roe on a well-provided mission to Jahangir's court in Agra in an attempt to negotiate more favourable terms of entry and trade for the English in India. This was to prove a turning point in the relationship between the two countries and would lead to the increasingly deep and complex involvement of the English, and later—after the

Act of Union with Scotland in 1707—the British, in the affairs of the subcontinent. As Roe set off on his delicate and tricky mission, however, such an outcome was far from certain.

2

'Infamous for their honest endeavours': Laying Foundations, 1615–1708

On his arrival at Agra, Sir Thomas Roe refused to admit any inferiority before the Emperor Jahangir: 'I passed on until I came to a place railed in right under him [Jahangir] with an ascent of three steps where I made him reverence and he bowed his body; and so went within it. I demanded a chair, but was answered no man ever sat in that place, but I was desired as a courtesy to ease myself against a pillar, covered with silver that held up his canopy.'[1]

In the end, Roe stayed at the Great Mughal's court for more than three years, trying to extract better trade terms for the East India Company. But it is also clear that Jahangir encouraged him to stay at least partly to satisfy his own curiosity with this proud alien being, rather as

European rulers were later to display exotic 'natives' from Africa at their own courts.

Roe did not altogether enjoy staying on at Agra, exclaiming, melodramatically 'I would sooner die than be subject to the slavery the Persian [ambassador] is content with'.[2] At last, Roe did obtain permission for the Company to open factories in certain Indian towns. This really made Surat a permanent base for English trade, and possibly for expansion. There seems no doubt that Roe's proud and dignified conduct reflected well on his nation, especially as the Company was beginning to demonstrate its sea power to the Indians.

However, Roe did not advocate that the Company enter upon wars of conquest in India. He argued that the Portuguese and the Dutch used up all their eastern profits in military adventures:

> It is the beggaring of the Portugal, notwithstanding his many rich residences and territories, that he keeps soldiers that spend it, yet his garrisons are mean. He never profited by the Indies, since he defended them. Observe this well. It hath been also the error of the Dutch, who seek plantation here by the sword. They turn a wonderful stock, they prowl in all places, they possess some of the best; yet their dead pays consume all their gain. Let this be received as a rule that if you will profit, seek it at sea, and in quiet trade; for without controversy, it is an error to affect garrisons and land wars in India.[3]

This advice, though no doubt prudent in the short term, was to prove impossible to follow as the rivalry between competing European powers hotted up during the early years of the eighteenth century. It did, however, illustrate a crucial aspect of the extension of English control in the region. Quite simply, it was often far more effective to negotiate deals with the Mughals or with local potentates than to rush in with guns blazing and swords flashing. Statecraft, and the patient playing-off of one group against another, was often an excellent and economical way forward. So was the encouragement of collaboration between a variety of Indian elites and groups with the English authorities. Indeed, it is arguable that, even at the height of its power, the Raj relied upon the collaboration of the ruled with the rulers just as much as upon military strength.

Before he left Agra in 1619, Roe also informed the Company that 'my sincerity toward you in all actions is without spot; my neglect of private gain is without example, and my frugality beyond your expectation'. Heartfelt as this piece of self-advertisement was, it went to the crux of what was to become one of the biggest problems for the East India Company for the next one-and-a-half centuries: the chronic conflict between Company interests and the venal self-interest of many of its senior servants. European corruption was to be endemic until the end of the eighteenth century.

From 1619, when Roe finally left Agra, until 1640, Surat was the chief base of the English in the East. In 1641, however, Francis Day, a Company representative in southern India, obtained from a local Hindu raja a strip of land on which was built the fortified factory of St George. From these small beginnings grew the great bastion of British power in south-east India—Madras, one of the most important cities of British India.

Shortly after the acquisition of Fort St George, events in England put the Company's activities in India into a minor key, when the growing conflict between Charles I and Parliament erupted in 1642 into Civil War and Revolution. Although under Cromwell's leadership the Commonwealth government in England pursued aggressive and vigorous colonial and commercial policies during the 1650s, they were chiefly aimed at expansion in the West Indies and North America—the much-vaunted 'Western design'.

The Commonwealth did, however, make real efforts to protect and encourage British shipping on a global scale. In the year of Charles I's trial and execution, 1649, Parliament passed a Navigation Act that was followed by a second, supplementary Act in 1660. As a result, all colonial trade had to be carried by British ships. In addition, in 1649, British ship-owners were given the legal right to protection by the British navy—a measure confirmed at the Restoration of the monarchy in 1660. From 1650, moreover, the administration embarked on a substantial ship-building programme, which also continued after the change of regime in 1660. Cromwell's aggressive policy towards the Netherlands led to the first Anglo-Dutch War (1652–4), where the successes of the fleet under Admiral Blake did a good deal to reduce the effectiveness of the Dutch as powerful naval and commercial rivals.

All this served to benefit, even if indirectly, the position of the East India Company. As a result, although the 1650s were not marked by any noteworthy expansion of the Company's activities in India, its standing was enhanced overall. Much had been consolidated. The scene was now set for expansion.

This expansion was to begin shortly after the Restoration of the monarchy in 1660. In 1661, Charles II married the Portuguese Princess Catherine of Braganza. At her marriage, Catherine brought Bombay, widely considered to be the finest port on the West Indian coast, as part of her dowry. Charles, chronically short of cash, both for himself and for the task of government, and unable to wring sufficient funds out of Parliament, decided in 1668 to rent Bombay to the East India Company.

Twenty years later, growing English commercial activity in the Ganges delta led to the founding in 1690 of the fortified factory of Fort St William. From this was to develop the enormously successful commercial and administrative centre of Calcutta. Although built amid the unhealthy, low-lying swamps of the delta, the city of Calcutta came to symbolize British power in the densely populated province of Bengal. More than this, Calcutta became the capital of British India, remaining so until the building of New Delhi in the early twentieth century. It also became a city of some architectural note, with grand British buildings aping European models—for example the churches of St John's and St Andrew's were modelled on St Martin-in-the Fields, the offices of the East India Railway Station on the Palazzo Farnese in Rome, and the High Court upon the Ypres Cloth Hall.

Within a century of its formation, the basic pattern of the East India Company's landholdings in the subcontinent was now clear. Three great and rapidly expanding centres of English and Company power had been established on the west and south-east coasts of India and on the Ganges delta. In between, however, lay a massive, often heavily populated hinterland, where Europeans were as strange as aliens from outer space and where Mughal and local princely power were paramount. For the Company to bring under its control even a modest part of the huge area that lay between its early landholdings seemed a daunting and even unnecessary task as the seventeenth century drew to a close.

Early English activities in India caused much controversy and comment at home. Indeed, this was to be the case for much of the time the British ruled India. The crux of the issue was, how did people from a windswept set of islands on the edge of the North Atlantic adapt to Indian conditions? Although some Company servants 'went native', especially in the seventeenth and eighteenth centuries, this was increasingly frowned upon as 'letting the side down' and as incompatible with the deportment of a ruling European elite.

In these circumstances, and especially at the outset, life for the Company's employees was often unpleasant and sometimes short. Englishmen in Surat or Madras or Calcutta continued to wear thick clothing, eat a heavy meal at midday, and drink too much wine.

One Company man complained that 'at home men are famous for doing nothing; here they are infamous for their honest endeavours. At home is respect and reward; abroad is disrespect and heartbreaking. At home is augmentation of wages; abroad no more than the third of wages. At home is content; abroad nothing so much as grief, cares and displeasure. At home is safety; abroad no security. At home is liberty; abroad the best is bondage.'[4]

In the early 1670s, in an attempt to improve some of their men's lives in Bombay—and perhaps to cut down on liaisons with Indian women—the East India Company sent out twenty single Englishwomen of 'sober and civil lives'. This experiment in marital and social engineering did not, however, go smoothly. The Company found that some of the women 'are grown scandalous to our nation, religion and government', and the proper authorities were told to 'give them all fair warning that they do apply themselves to a more sober and Christian conversation, otherwise the sentence is this, that they shall be confined totally of their liberty to go abroad, and fed with bread and water till they are embarked on board ship for England'.[5]

Of course, Bombay was not the only den of iniquity. In 1676 the Company's chaplain in Madras wrote a scandalized letter to the directors concerning the moral state of the English community there:

> I have the charity to believe that most of you have so much zeal for God, and for the credit of religion, that your heads would be fountains of water, and eyes rivers of tears, did you really know how much God is dishonoured, his name blasphemed . . . by the vicious lives of many of your servants. . . .
>
> I do earnestly wish there may be more inspection taken what persons you send over into these places; for there come hither some thousand murderers, some men stealers, some popish, some come over under the notion of single persons and unmarried, who yet have their wives in England, and here have lived in adultery. . . . Some on the other hand have come over as married [couples] of whom there are strange suspicions they were never married. . . .
>
> Others pride themselves in making others drink till they be insensible, and then strip them naked, and in that posture cause them to be carried through the streets to their dwelling place. Some of them, with other persons whom they invited, once went abroad to a garden not far off, and there continued a whole day and night drinking most

excessively, and in so much that one of the number died within a very few days after.[6]

This was hardly the way in which to construct an image of a godly, righteous, and responsible alien minority. If the conduct of some of the Company's servants aroused debate, so too did the matter of conducting the steadily increasing volume of trade with India. The essential problem was that English-made goods were not always easy to exchange for Indian merchandise. As a result, the Company had to plug the trade gap between imports and exports by paying for some Indian goods in silver bullion. This was fundamentally an unsatisfactory commercial and financial relationship, and was a long way from the imperial ideal of an efficient trading system.

The economic and social problems raised by Indian trade were cogently and plainly expressed in the late 1600s by the MP Henry Martyn. It was an argument that went to the heart of the problem, and gives a very clear picture of the nature of the commercial relationship between England and India:

> There is no reason, that the Indians will take off any of our manufacturers, as long as there is such a difference in the price of English and Indian labour, as long as the labour or manufacture of the East Indies shall be valued there at but one-sixth part of the price of like labour or manufacture here in England. . . . Therefore, unless now and then for curiosities, English manufacturers will seldom go to India.

Without the help of laws, we shall have little reason to expect any other returns for our bullion, than only manufactures, for these will be most profitable. For the freight of unwrought things from India is equal to the freight of so much manufacture; the freight of a pound of cotton is equal to so much callico [*sic*]; the freight of raw silk to that of wrought silk. But the labour by which this cotton or raw silk is to be wrought in England is a great deal dearer than the labour by which the same would be wrought in India.

Therefore of all things which can be imported thence, manufactures are bought cheapest; they will be most demanded here, the chief returns will be on these. Little then will be returned from India besides manufactures. And when these shall be imported here they will be likely to stay. In France, Venice, and other countries, Indian manufactures are prohibited. The great consumption must be in England.

It has been proved by arguments that bullion and chiefly bullion is carried into India, that chiefly manufactures must be returned, and that these must be consumed in England. But instead of all other arguments, is matter of fact: cargoes of bullion are every year carried into India, while almost every one at home is seen in Indian manufactures. . . .

The next complaint against this trade is of the labourer: that he is driven from his employment to beg his bread; by the permission of Indian manufactures to come to England, English manufactures must be lost.[7]

If the Company had remained limited in its trading ambitions, or if the English government had been, in either the medium or the long term, unwilling to legislate in order to aid British merchants, these misgivings would have been far more weighty.

Since, however, the Company continued to diversify its commercial activities in the East—beginning to trade in China tea in 1700, for example—the early problems of commerce with India were less painful than they might have been. As it was, the first century of the East India Company's commercial history was one of fairly steady, if unspectacular, progress.

The political and military position of the Company, however, remained precarious. For one thing, there was Portuguese and Dutch hostility towards what they saw as English interlopers. For another, there was the gradual disintegration of Mughal power that began during the reign of the Emperor Aurangzeb (1658–1707). As a symptom of Mughal decline, Shivaji, the great Maratha leader, began to assert his independence in west-central India. For a time the Maratha Confederacy was to achieve a paramount position in India.

The prestige of Shivaji rivalled that of the Great Mughal himself, as can be seen in a description of the former's coronation in 1674:

> The coverings of the royal seat were a grotesque combination of ancient Hindu asceticism and modern Mogul luxury: tiger skin below and velvet on top. On the two sides of the throne various emblems of royalty and government were hung from gilded lance-heads. On the right

stood two large fish-heads of gold with very big teeth, and on the left several horses' tails (the insignia of royalty among the Turks) and a pair of gold scales, evenly balanced (the emblem of justice) on a very costly lance-head. All these were copied from the Mogul Court. At the palace gate were placed on either hand pitchers full of water covered with bunches of leaves, and also two young elephants and two beautiful horses, with gold bridles and rich trappings. These were auspicious tokens according to Hindu ideas.[8]

It was soon apparent that not only was the Company's position at Surat, Bombay, and Madras threatened by the growing anarchy, but that Calcutta was at risk, too. Understandably, the directors of the Company were anxious to appoint men of high calibre and sophisticated education during these hazardous times.

Interestingly, when in 1687 they chose a new member of the Council for Madras (or Fort St George), they insisted that he should be 'a man of learning, and competently well read in ancient histories of the Greeks and Latins, which with a good stock of natural parts only can render a man fit for government and political science, martial prudence and other requisites to rule over a great city. . . . For its not being bred a boy in India, or staying long there and speaking the language or understanding critically the trade of the place, that is sufficient to fit a man for such a command as the Second of Fort St George is, or may be, in time, though all these qualifications are very good in their kind.'[9]

Even outstanding and good men could do little without proper support from home. It was therefore perhaps inevitable that, amid the decline of Mughal power, persuasive voices began to demand a policy of military consolidation in India. Some idea of how poorly things were beginning to go for the Company as subcontinental power structures began to collapse may be gauged from the description of the pitiful state of Bengal in 1678 by an English observer, Job Charnock: 'The whole Kingdom is lying in a very miserable feeble condition, the great ones plundering and robbing the feebler.'[10]

There was no shortage of those offering a cure to the perceived malady. A Company man, Gerald Aungier, argued that:

> The state of India . . . is much altered of what it was; that justice and respect, wherewith strangers in general and especially those of our nation were wont to be treated with, is quite laid aside; the name of the honourable Company and the English nation through our long patient sufferings of wrong, is become slighted; our complaints, remonstrances, paper protests, and threatenings are laughed at. . . . In violent distempers violent cures are only successful . . . the times now require you to manage your general commerce with your sword in your hands.[11]

The sword was indeed to play a far larger and more significant part in furthering the fortunes of the East India Company.

Not all threats to the Company, however, came from India itself. After William of Orange's accession to the English throne, in partnership with his wife Queen Mary Stuart, after the Glorious Revolution of 1688, he allowed the formation of a New East India Company in 1698.

Soon other traders were being given a free hand in Indian commerce. The old and the new East India Companies competed briefly, and not very profitably, with each other. Finally, just as England and Scotland became a unified state in 1707, an amalgamation seemed the only sensible solution. In 1708 the United Company of Merchants of England Trading to the East Indies was formed. It was this body, inexorably growing in power and territory, that was to last for almost 150 years, until the cataclysm of the great Indian rebellion of 1857–8.

3

Conquest and Corruption: The Struggle for Supremacy, 1708–1815

In a little over a century, Britain, through the agency of the East India Company, became the dominant European power in the subcontinent. The wars against France and its allies that raged for much of the eighteenth century were in effect world wars. The spoils for the victors were nothing less than global commercial, trading, naval, and imperial supremacy. Not even the military genius of Napoleon was able to thwart British war aims. The end of the French Republican and Napoleonic Wars in 1815 was therefore an extraordinary moment of truth for both British and French overseas destinies.

How had this remarkable triumph happened? Not only had the British East Company contained, and eventually destroyed, the challenge of the French East India Company, but it had also pushed aside the Dutch and the Portuguese in the struggle for commercial mastery. By 1815 other European powers merely held small pieces of Indian territory: the Portuguese had Goa, Daman, and Diu; the French had Pondicherry, Mahé, Chandernagore, Yanaon, and Karikal.

These bases might have posed a military threat to the British, but the supremacy of the Royal Navy, and the generally effective support of the home government, helped to ensure the eventual triumph of Britain's interests. The British also proved skilful at constructing alliances with local rulers and in thus advancing their interests through a potent combination of military power and statecraft.

The struggle for mastery was never easy. During the eighteenth century Britain fought France three times for supremacy in India. The first struggle came during the War of the Austrian Succession (1740–8); the next was an unofficial war in India from 1750 to 1754; the final and conclusive conflict came during the Seven Years War (1756–63).

Until the early 1750s the French were doing relatively well in the confrontation. The dynamic and determined Governor of Pondicherry, Dupleix (Governor 1742–54), made a flying start in the struggle for power, and it was not until Robert Clive emerged from obscurity as a soldier of genius that the balance tilted in favour of the British.

Clive, who was Governor of Bengal in 1757–60, and again in 1765–7, finally crushed the French and their Indian allies in that province at the great Battle of Plassey in 1757. More than any other victory, Plassey marked a practical and symbolic triumph that guaranteed the future for Britain in India.

The triumph at Plassey brought the large, commercially valuable and heavily populated province of Bengal under the rule of the East India Company. By 1818 the British had also turned on and defeated the major Indian power, the Maratha Confederacy, and had reduced the Mughal Emperor in Delhi to the status of a puppet ruler without any real authority. This was the final confirmation of Britain's subcontinental supremacy.

It was not, however, easy. It took three gruelling wars to break the Maratha Confederacy. But the Marathas had often made enemies among large sections of the Indian people through their ruthless raiding and looting, an often horrifying process, as described by a Bengali poet:

> The bargis [horsemen] came up and encircled them [the fleeing villagers] in the plain. They snatched away gold and silver, rejecting all else. Of some people they cut off the hand, of some the nose and ears; some they killed outright. They dragged away the beautiful women, tying their fingers to their necks with ropes. . . .
>
> After looting in the open, the bargis entered the villages. They set fire to the houses, large and small, temples and dwelling places. After burning the villages they roamed on

all sides plundering. Some victims they tied with their arms twisted behind them. Some they flung down and kicked with their shoes. They constantly shouted, 'Give us rupees, give us rupees, give us rupees!' When they got no rupees, they filled their victims nostrils with water and drowned them in tanks. Some were put to death by suffocation. Those who had money gave it to the bargis; those who had none gave up their lives.[1]

The slow, inexorable decline in the power and standing of the Mughal Empire was completed by the start of the nineteenth century. Two descriptions of the Emperor Alam separated by half a century give a vivid picture of the process. In the mid-eighteenth century the Frenchman Jean Law described Shah Alam, who was crowned Emperor in 1759, thus:

> The Shahzada passed for one of those who have had the best education and who have most profited by it. This education consists particularly in the knowledge of religion; of the Oriental tongues, and of history, and in the writing of one's academic exercises well. In effect, all that I could perceive decided in his favour. He is familiar with the Arabic, Persian, Turki [sic], and Hindustani languages. He loves reading and never passes a day without employing some hours in it. . . . He is of an enquiring mind, naturally gay and free in his private society, where he frequently admits his principal military officers in whom he has confidence.[2]

By 1803 Shah Alam, now an old man with his former glory stripped from him, saw the British march into Delhi: 'At length the Commander-in-Chief was ushered into the royal presence, and found the unfortunate and venerable Emperor, oppressed by the accumulated calamities of old age, degraded authority, extreme poverty, and loss of sight, seated under a small tattered canopy, the remnant of his royal state, with every external appearance of the misery of his condition.'[3]

While the British East India Company was asserting its control over indigenous people and pushing aside its European rivals, it also suffered a crisis of conscience over its standards of administration. The basic problem was how to control the widespread corruption of Company officials. When faced, as they were from the outset, with a system of chronic bribery and corruption in India, the servants of the Company had frequently used the same methods in their dealings with Indians. It was perhaps all part of the tendency for some British men during the seventeenth and much of the eighteenth centuries to 'go native.'

These problems had been brought dramatically to the public's attention during Warren Hastings's Governorship of India, in 1773–85. Ironically, Hastings had been sent out to India to end corruption. He had to return to England, however, to face charges that he had himself been guilty of the same misdemeanours.

It gives some idea of the ethos of Company service towards the end of the eighteenth century that, because

Hastings had been constantly criticized by one of his advisers, Philip Francis, in 1781, he felt obliged to fight a duel with him. This was a rumbustious and individualistic approach to Indian administration that was a far reach from the orderly team work that was to charactize the Victorian Indian Civil Service.

Hastings left a vivid account of the confrontation:

> His pistol went off at the time, and so near the same instant that I am not certain which was first, but believe mine was first and that his followed in the instant. He staggered immediately, his face expressed a sensation of being struck, and his limbs shortly but gradually went under him, and he fell saying, but not loudly, 'I am dead.'
> I ran to him, shocked, I own, at the information. . . . The Seconds also ran to his assistance. I saw his coat pierced on the right side, and feared the ball had passed through him; but he sat up without much difficulty several times and once attempted with our help to stand, but his limbs failed him and he sank to the ground. Colonel W. then proposed that as we had met from a point of honour and not for personal rancour, we should join hands. . . . We did so, Mr. F. cheerfully; and I expressed my regret at the condition to which I saw him reduced.[4]

Warren Hastings sailed for home convinced that, despite these controversies, he had made British rule in India secure. On board ship he wrote: 'I have saved India, in spite of them all, from foreign conquest. . . . [I have] become the instrument of raising the British name, and the substantial worth of its possessions in India, to a degree of prosperity proportioned to such a trust. [Yet both have vanished] in an instant, like the illusions of a dream, with the poor and only consolation left me of the conscious knowledge of what I could have effected, had my destiny ordained it.'[5]

In 1788, three years after returning home, Hastings was impeached—that is, brought to trial—before the House of Lords. The great Parliamentarian Edmund Burke led the attack on him. The impeachment dragged on from 1788 to 1795. In the end, Hastings was acquitted of the charges brought against him for his administration in India. But his reputation and fortune had by now vanished. Only towards the end of his life was his work in India seen in its true, and more kindly, light.

The impeachment of Hastings can be seen as part of a large and more important debate about the purpose of the Company's rule in India. Millions of non-European subjects had been acquired with the annexation of Bengal: should commercial interests dominate the Company's policy-making? Or did British administrators have a duty to protect their Indian subjects and to improve the quality of their lives? This notion in turn fed into the concept of the 'civilizing mission', which was to become so central to the spread and organization of the British Empire worldwide.

As a result of these preoccupations, the British State came to play a larger part in the Company's affairs. In 1773

Parliament passed the Regulating Act, which named a Governor General for Bengal, aided by four advisers, who was able to supervise the Governors of Bombay and Madras.

The Regulating Act, however, was a fairly feeble measure of intervention. A decade later, in 1783, Charles James Fox, the great Whig reformer, introduced his India Bill. The purpose of Fox's Bill was to attempt to give Parliament greater control over the administration in British India, while leaving commercial matters to the Company. After much political in-fighting, and the open and predictable hostility of King George III, the Bill was rejected in the House of Lords, helping to cause the collapse of the Fox–North coalition government.

The new government was led by William Pitt the younger, son of the great Earl of Chatham, and now Prime Minister at the age of 24. Pitt presented his own India Bill in 1784, and it became law the same year. It shared many of the features of Fox's India Bill. A Board of Control, responsible to Parliament, was set up. The Bill also gave Indian subjects of the Company equality before the law. Thus, not only had the State taken another large step towards control of administration in India, but it had asserted, perhaps a little indirectly, that Britain had a moral duty towards its Indian subjects and a responsibility for their welfare. The tricky bit was what would happen when the interests of British commerce and imperialism clashed with the interests of the indigenous population. None-theless, this 'Dual Control' of Parliament and Company lasted until the Indian rebellion or Mutiny of 1857.

Despite these reforms, the East India Company remained an enormously influential body, even though its trading activities by 1800 were less extensive and successful than fifty years before. The vessels of 'John Company' continued to plough a stately and generally comfortable passage, laden on the home trip with cargoes of tea, silks, chinaware, and muslin.

An idea of what this process was like was provided by Captain Eastwick, a Company man, who wrote:

These vessels were especially built for the service, and were generally run for about four voyages, when they were held to be worn out, and their places taken by others built for the purpose. About thirty ships were required for the company every year. . . .

The captain of an East Indiaman, in addition to his pay and allowances, had the right of free outward freight to the extent of fifty tons, being only debarred from exporting certain articles, such as woollens, metals, and warlike stores. On the homeward voyage he was allotted twenty tons of free freight, each of thirty-two feet; but this tonnage was bound to consist of certain scheduled goods, and duties were payable thereon to the company. . . .

The gains to a prudent commander averaged from £4,000 to £5,000 a voyage, sometimes perhaps falling as low as £2,000, but at others rising to £10,000 or £12,000. The time occupied from the period of a ship commencing receipt of her outward cargo to her being finally cleared of her homeward one was generally from fourteen to eighteen months, and three or four voyages assured any man a very handsome fortune.[6]

In India itself, officials and merchants grappled with problems of enormous complexity. Among the most intractable of these was the recurrence of famine. In 1769–70 famine struck Bengal hard:

> The husbandmen sold their cattle; they sold their implements of agriculture; they devoured their seed grain; they sold their sons and their daughters, till at length no buyer of children could be found; they ate the leaves of trees and the grass of the field; and in June 1770 the Resident at the Durbar affirmed that the living were feeding on the dead.
>
> Day and night a torrent of famished and disease-stricken wretches poured into the great cities. At an early period of the year pestilence had broken out. In March we find smallpox at Moorshedabad, where it glided through the Viceregal mutes and cut off the Prince Syfut in his palace. Interment could not do its work quick enough, even the dogs and jackals, the public scavengers of the East, became unable to accomplish their revolting work, and the multitude of mangled and festering corpses at length threatened the existence of the citizens.[7]

Another problem, arising from the desperate poverty in which so many Indians lived, was slavery. This curse went on, despite Lord Cornwallis's attack on it in 1789, during his governor generalship. In 1785, Sir William Jones, Chief Judge of the Supreme Court, wrote:

Hardly a man or woman exists in a corner of this populous town who hath not at least one slave child, either purchased at a trifling price or saved for a life that seldom fails of being miserable. Many of you, I presume, have seen large boats filled with such children coming down the river for open sale at Calcutta. Nor can you be ignorant that most of them were stolen from their parents or bought for perhaps a measure of rice, in time of scarcity.[8]

Inevitably, Indian society, with its extremes of fabulous wealth and unspeakable poverty, and with the rigid caste system of the Hindu religion, invited varied reactions from British observers. There were those like the administrator Charles Grant who wrote: 'We cannot avoid recognising in the people of Hindostan a race of men lamentably degenerate and base; retaining but a feeble sense of moral obligation; yet obstinate in their disregard of what they know to be right, governed by malevolent and licentious passions, strongly exemplifying the effects produced on society by a great and general corruption of manners.'[9]

Even a progressive thinker, like James Mill, the British philosopher, dismissed Indian law as 'a disorderly compilation of loose, vague, stupid or unintelligible quotations and maxims selected arbitrarily from books of law, books of devotion, and books of poetry; attended with a commentary which only adds to the absurdity and darkness; a farrago by which nothing is defined, nothing established'.[10]

Of course, Mill's strictures were chiefly aimed at what he perceived as a backward, confused, and reactionary legal system. It was commonplace, however, for both British liberals and conservatives to criticize Indian ways and means. These low opinions of the Indian people had the effect of projecting onto them as the 'other' a mass of undesirable, even ludicrous characteristics. This in its turn served to justify British rule as a benevolent, indeed necessary, thing.

British anxieties about India had found popular justification in the infamous incident of the 'Black Hole of Calcutta', during the Seven Years War. After forces under the Bengali ruler Siraj-ad-daula had captured Calcutta, some 140 Britons had been locked up in grossly cramped conditions. By the morning, 123 of them had died of suffocation.

A contemporary account recounted what happened, though perhaps in overdramatic terms:

> Observing every one giving way to the violence of passions, which I foresaw must be fatal to them, I requested silence might be preserved, whilst I spoke to them, and in the most pathetic and moving terms . . . I begg'd and intreated, that as they had paid a ready obedience to me in the day, they would now for their own sakes and the sakes of those who were dear to them, and were interested in the preservation of their lives, regard the advice I had to give them.
>
> I assured them, the return of day would give us air and liberty; urged to them, that the only chance we had left for

sustaining this misfortune, and surviving the night, was the preserving [of] a calm mind and quiet resignation to our fate. [I intreated] them to curb, as much as possible, every agitation of mind and body, as raving and giving loose to their passions could answer no purpose, but that of hastening their destruction. . . . Various expedients were thought of to give more room and air. To obtain the former, it was moved to put off their clothes. This was approved as a happy motion, and in a few minutes I believe every man was stripped.

For a little time they flattered themselves with having gained a mighty advantage. Every hat was put in motion to produce a circulation of air, and Mr Baillie proposed that every man should sit down on his hams. As they were truly in the situation of drowning wretches, no wonder they caught at every thing that bore a flattering appearance of saving them. This expedient was several times put in practice, and at each time many of the poor creatures whose natural strength was less than others, or had been more exhausted and could not immediately recover their legs, as others did when the word was given to rise, fell to rise no more. For they were instantly trod to death or suffocated.

When the whole body sat down, they were so closely wedged together that they were obliged to use many efforts before they could put themselves in motion to get up again. Before nine o'clock every man's thirst grew intolerable.[11]

This catastrophic incident probably owed more to Indian carelessness than to deliberate cruelty and malice; nonetheless it lived on in British history as an example of barbarism, fuelling and confirming prejudice.

Unfortunately, the reforming work of British missionaries, and the sympathetic attitudes of many British administrators, may have had far less impact on the imagination of the average British citizen. But just as there were those who criticized Indian society, there were those who believed that the beliefs and customs of that society should, in general, be respected.

The routine and life of the average British administrator in the Company's service were often hard and monotonous, despite the financial rewards and the power that could be exercised. The Marquis of Wellesley, Governor General from 1798 to 1805, described his lonely life:

Without my wife, I fear, I shall not have fortitude to remain here long enough to accomplish my grand financial, military, naval, commercial, architectural, judicial, political reforms, and to make up a large treasure. . . . All this might be effected within five or six years from the day of my embarkation at Cowes. But I leave you to judge of the necessity of her society while I give you some idea of my private life.

I rise early and go out before breakfast, which is always between eight and nine. From that hour until four, in the hot weather, I remain at work, unless I go to the Council, or to church on Sundays. At five I dine, and drive out in the evening. No constitution here can bear the sun in the middle of the day any season of the year, nor the labour of the business in the evening. After dinner, therefore, nobody attempts to write or read, and, in general, it is thought necessary to avoid even meetings on subjects of business at that time; for in this climate good or ill health depends upon a minute attention to circumstances apparently the most trivial. Thus, in the evening I have no alternative but the society of my subjects, or solitude. The former is so vulgar, ignorant, rude, familiar, and stupid as to be disgusting and intolerable; especially the ladies, not one of whom, by-the-bye, is even decently good-looking.

The greatest inconvenience, however, arises from the ill-bred familiarity of the general manners. . . . The effect of this state of things on my conduct has been to compel me to entrench myself within forms and ceremonies, to introduce as much state into the whole appearance of my establishments and household, to expel all approaches to familiarity, and to exercise my authority with a degree of vigour and strictness nearly amounting to severity.

It required some unpleasant efforts to place matters on this footing, and you must perceive that I am forced to fly to solitude for a large portion of the twenty-four hours, lest I should weaken my means of performing my public duty.[12]

Lord Cornwallis, Governor General from 1786 to 1793, was also under no illusions over his working day:

I get on horse-back just as the dawn of day begins to appear, ride on the same road and the same distance, pass the whole forenoon after my return from riding in doing business, and almost exactly the same portion of time every day at table, drive out in a phaeton [light four-wheeled carriage] a little before sunset, then write or read over letters or papers on business for two hours. Sit down

at nine with two or three officers of my family to some fruit
and a biscuit and go to bed soon after the clock strikes ten.
I don't think that the greatest sap [swot] at Eton can lead a
duller life than this.[13]

Throughout the Company, officials of lesser rank found
ways of breaking the boredom. Heavy drinking was one
way to achieve oblivion, but insubordinate behaviour and
gambling were also commonplace. In 1711 the behaviour of
some junior Company men at Fort St George at Madras
was the subject of concern:

> We are sorry to hear that of late there has not been a suffi-
> cient decorum kept up among our people, and particularly
> among the young writers and factors, that there have been
> files of musketeers sent for to keep the peace at dinner
> time. . . . We direct that you the President and Council, do
> at certain stated seasons set apart a time to enquire into the
> behaviour of all our factors and writers . . . and calling them
> severally before you, let them know the account you have
> of them, and as they deserve either admonish or command
> them. . . . It lies very much in your power to form their
> minds to virtue.[14]

In 1717 heavy drinking at the distant settlement of Ben-
coolen in Sumatra provoked another firm and disapproving dispatch from the Company's directors:

> Could we once hear sobriety was become as fashionable on
> the West Coast as hard drinking hath been, we should
> entertain strong hopes that your new settlement at Marl-
> borough . . . would give a better reputation to the West

Coast than it hath hitherto had on account of health. . . . it is positively affirmed you have good water, if you will be at the pains of fetching what is so. It is further said that a little tea boiled in the water doth admirably correct it, and that water kept till cold and so drank as water would contribute to the health of those who used it.[15]

A few years later in 1721 the directors were expressing their anxiety over the extent of gambling at Fort St George:

It is with great concern we hear the itch of gaming hath spread itself over Madras, that even the gentle-women play for great sums, and that Capt. Seaton makes a trade of it to the stripping several of the young men there. We earnestly recommend to you to check as far as you can that mischievous evil. Let Capt. Seaton know if he continues that vicious practice he shall not stay but be removed, and do you take care he be sent off the shore . . . and civilly acquaint the gentle-women that we desire they will put a stop to all high gaming, because first or last it will be prejudicial and ruinous to them or theirs.[16]

It is unlikely that these high-minded and earnest exhortations had much effect upon bored, comparatively wealthy roisterers half the world away from Britain. Nonetheless, the East India Company kept up a flow of sober advice for those who bore the growing burden of administration during the eighteenth century.

Dispatches to Bengal and St Helena, sent in 1714 and in 1717, set a tone that would not have been out of place at the high noon of the Victorian Raj: 'We have always recommended to you to see justice administered impartially to all and speedily, to govern mildly and yet preserve authority. We have reason to add it here again for your remembrance, and earnestly to desire you will take care none under you be suffered to insult the natives, and that no voice of oppression be heard in your streets, this is the best method to enlarge our towns and increase our revenues.'[17]

The dispatches continued to strike a moral high note: 'Never do an act of arbitrary power to hurt anybody. Let your determinations be always just, not rigorous but inclining to the merciful side. Always try the cause, never the Party. Don't let passion overcloud your reason. This will make the people respect you whereas one violent sentence or action will sully the reputation of ten good ones.'[18]

There is little doubt that such advice was self-serving as well as ethically correct. British rule was aimed at the continuing and increasing domination of the subcontinent. What better way to encourage this process than by convincing Indians that European administration was essentially just and fair minded, and certainly better than the rule of their own people might be? All the same, these were not easy standards to live up to during the eighteenth century.

4

'The great ends we have in view': The East India Company as Paramount Power, 1815–1857

Although the Company's subcontinental supremacy was affirmed by the ending of the Third Maratha War in 1818, this triumph did not bring universal peace to India or usher in an era of tranquillity. In fact, right up to the outbreak of the great rebellion of 1857, the territory of the East India Company was being steadily extended, until over two-thirds of the whole were under British control.

It is true that these annexations were not always the result of long-term planning by the British, the result of imperialist plots hatched in smoke-filled rooms. Instead, territorial expansion was frequently a response to the various pressures put upon the Company—commercial, financial, military, strategic, and so forth. Sometimes the response was reluctant; sometimes it was rash or spontaneous. At other times, some shift in the circumstances presented the British with a window of opportunity to further their interests through military action or through negotiation and treaty. Often it was local circumstances that were more significant than countrywide ones. In any event, the East India Company's need to hold, defend, and consolidate existing territory encouraged an overwhelmingly 'forward' policy of expansion.

Even if the Company was slow to begin some of its wars of conquest, the final count of military campaigns and conquests between 1818 and 1857 is little short of awe inspiring: 1824–6 the First Burma War; 1839–42 First Afghan War; 1843 Sind conquered; 1844 defeat of the province of Gwalior; 1845–6 First Sikh War; 1848–9 Second Sikh War, by which the whole of the Punjab was annexed; 1852 Second Burma War, leading to the annexation of the whole of Burma. Nagpur was annexed in 1853, and Avadh, or Oudh, in 1856. In addition, other minor provinces were also brought under the Company's rule.

Although by 1856 almost 70 per cent of the subcontinent had fallen to the British, what was the position of the remaining provinces—the India still ruled by the princes? The arrangements here showed the British at their most pragmatic and, in a way, skilful. Rather than waste precious resources in yet more wars of conquest, some of which might have had uncertain outcomes, the East India Company decided to draw up treaties by which the princes enjoyed a theoretical autonomy, but were in fact dominated by Britain, especially in terms of their external relations.

These arrangements suited both sides. The princes could keep their wealth and their privileges, their palaces and their harems, their jewels and their hunting elephants; they could continue to rule their subjects, providing they did not treat them so badly as to offend British notions of reasonably good government. The British had no need to take over yet more territory and set up complex administrative systems, but could count on the cooperation and support of the princes when it mattered. Just to make sure, a British Resident was appointed to each significant Indian principality, to act as a channel of communications and to keep an eye on the local ruler.

The princely states varied enormously in size and importance. Some were merely a few square miles of territory, but others were equivalent to whole countries—Hyderabad, for example, was bigger than Spain. The arrangement had its negative side for many millions of the Indian princes' subjects, who were nearly all denied the comparatively impartial administration and the sometimes beneficial impact of the economic development of British India.

Too often the Indian princes swaggered like self-indulgent medieval monarchs within their kingdoms, lords of all they surveyed. Some did try to follow British standards of administration, sent their sons to Oxford and Cambridge, and took up cricket—sometimes, as in the case of Prince Ranjitsinhji (1872–1933), playing the rulers' classical game so well that a British commentator noted: 'Here was a black man playing cricket not as a white man but as an artist of another and superior strain.'

Especially in the aftermath of the uprising, or 'mutiny', of 1857–8, the British came to rely increasingly on the loyalty and goodwill of their princely collaborators. For their part, the princes hitched their futures to British rule in such a way as to give them little room for manœuvre in the face of the rise of Indian nationalism from the late nineteenth century. In fact, so deeply did many princes fear the increasingly democratic activities of the Congress movement during the twentieth century that they banned it from their states.

All of this, however, was for the future. Between the end of the Napoleonic Wars and the outbreak of the great rebellion in 1857, the East India Company continued to flex its muscles with little fear of reverses. Indeed, apart from the disastrous invasion of Afghanistan in 1839, the campaigns of the East India Company's armies had been almost universally triumphant. Some had even given rise to poetry in the stolid and Victorian-heroic mould:

THE FIELD OF FEROZSHAH
(First Sikh War, 1845)

Our wounded lay upon the ground,
But little help was nigh,
No lint or bandage for the wound!
They laid them down to die.
Their wounds unstaunch'd, with cold and thirst
Our heroes suffered then the worst
Upon that fatal plain.
Many a man whose wounds were slight
Thro' the fell horrors of that night
Will never fight again.

. . . . .

At length our gallant cavalry
Scarce fifteen hundred men,
The flower of Britain's chivalry
Prepare to charge again.
That gallant chieftain Colonel White,
These heroes bravely led;
They sought the hottest of the fight,
Their path was strewn with dead.
'Twas plainly marked for all to see
Where charged our British cavalry.

By a young soldier (Sergeant Bingham)
who fought in that glorious campaign
(London, 1848)

A somewhat more chilling insight into the perils of
fighting the Afghans—something the British were to undertake with very mixed success three times between 1839 and

1921—can be found in Rudyard Kipling's poem 'The Young British Soldier':

> When you're wounded and left on Afghanistan's plains,
> And the women come out to cut up what remains,
> Jest roll to your rifle and blow out your brains
> An' go to your death like a soldier,
> Go, go, go like a soldier,
> Go, go, go like a soldier,
> Go, go, go like a soldier,
> So-oldier *of* the Queen![1]

The keenly contested Sikh Wars and the disastrous First Afghan War aside, however, the armies of the East India Company, increasingly dependant upon the tens of thousands of Indian mercenaries in their ranks, had little difficulty in subduing local resistance. Overwhelmingly, the superiority of Western military technology, organization, and supply was sufficient to do the job.

Once conquests had been achieved, however, a challenging set of problems and choices had to be faced. Chief among them was the fundamental question, how were these newly acquired subjects to be treated—Baluchis, Sikhs, Punjabis, and the rest? On the positive side, the British could take comfort from the widespread extent of collaboration and from the swarming, eager 'native' recruits into the Company's armies, and even increasingly admire the military prowess of the north-west frontier tribes, as well as being relieved at the stoic and generally passive qualities of village India. There were, however, less obedient subjects in the making in the great towns and cities. A growing number of newly educated, 'Westernized' Indians might be especially troublesome if they found British rule distasteful. In the early nineteenth century, however, these problems were a long way off.

As Company power grew, social contacts between British and Indians lessened as the nineteenth century unfolded. Indian princes and dignitaries, of course, were still quite acceptable to the British as both hosts and guests. Early in the century, the Mughul court and the leading lights of British society in Old Delhi mixed at official afternoon receptions. An Englishwoman described the Indian guests:

> A perfect bevy of princes, suave, watchful, ready at the slightest encouragement to crowd round the Resident, or the Commissioner, or the Brigadier, with noiseless white-stockinged feet. Equally ready to relapse into indifference when unnoticed.

> Here was Mirza Mughal, the king's eldest son, and his two supporters, all with lynx eyes for a sign, a hint, of favour or disfavour. And here—a sulky sickly looking lad of eighteen—was [Jivan Bakht], the queen's darling, dressed gorgeously and blazing with jewels which left no doubt as to who would be the heir-apparent if she had her way. Prince (Abu Bakr), however, scented, effeminate, watched the proceedings with bright eyes; giving the ladies unabashed admiration and after a time actually strolling away to listen to the music. Finally however, drifting

to the stables to gamble with the grooms over a quail fight.

Then there were lesser lights. [Ahsanullah Khan] the physician, his lean plausible face and thin white beard suiting his black gown and skull-cap, discussed the system of Greek medicine with the Scotch surgeon, whose fluent, trenchant Hindustani had an Aberdonian twang. . . . A few rich bankers curiously obsequious to the youngest ensign, and one or two pensioners owing their invitations to loyal service made up the company.[2]

In Kanpur (Cawnpore), in the province of Avadh (Oudh), the Nana Sahib entertained generously, dispensing pork, a meat strictly forbidden to Muslims, and displaying European gadgets and wares that caused some amusement among his British guests. The latter

sat down to a table twenty foot long (it had originally been the mess table of a cavalry regiment), which was covered with a damask table-cloth of European manufacture, but instead of a dinner napkin there was a bedroom towel. The soup . . . was served up in a trifle-dish which had formed part of a dessert service belonging to the 9th Lancers—at all events, the arms of that regiment were upon it; but the plate into which I ladled it with a broken teacup was of the old willow pattern. The pilao [rice dish] which followed the soup was served upon a huge plated dish, but the plate from which I ate was of the very commonest description. The knife was a bone-handled affair; the spoon and the fork were of silver, and of Calcutta make. The plated side-dishes, containing vegetables, were odd ones; one was round, the other oval.

The pudding was brought in upon a soup-plate of blue and gold pattern, and the cheese was placed before me on a glass dish belonging to a dessert service. The cool claret I drank out of a richly-cut champagne glass, and the beer out of an American tumbler, of the very worst quality.[3]

Indian nizams, rajahs, and maharajahs were, however, inevitably limited in number. Also, as more British women came out to join their menfolk, the British communities in India became more and more self-sufficient, more sealed off from non-European society. In the seventeenth and eighteenth centuries British men had often married, or, more commonly, lived with, Indian women. This practice, which had produced quite large numbers of children of mixed blood, was officially frowned upon at the end of the eighteenth century and rapidly declined from the early nineteenth century onwards. The Eurasian community, sometimes described as 'Anglo-Indian', that was the bi-product of these unions occupied an awkward place in Indian society, often feeling superior to mere 'natives' on account of their European blood, but at the same time not being accepted as equals by 'pukkah' British families.

In the more remote areas of India, though, inter-racial sexual contact still took place, and was mostly disap-proved of and criticized: 'When a man in office is under the power of a native woman, she invariably takes bribes, and he gets the credit for doing so; for she of course gives out that the Sahib shares in her extortions. . . . Now, putting the principles of morality out of the question, it is evident that an officer who thus places himself into the hands of a Heathen woman, is wholly unfit for any situation of authority.'[4]

As their numbers grew, and their self-confidence blossomed, British women in India became notorious for their gossip. The passing-on of juicy bits of scandal became a pastime for many, almost an art:

> In other parts of the world they talk about things, here they talk about people. The conversation is all personal, and, as such, you may be sure tolerably abusive. What did they find to say about one another? The veriest trifles in the world. Nothing is so insignificant as the staple of Calcutta conversation. What Mr This said to Miss That, and what Miss That did to Mr This. And then all the interminable gossip about marriages and no-marriages, and will-be marriages and ought-to-be marriages, and gentlemen's attention and ladies' flirtings, dress, reunions, and the last burrakhana [big dinner].[5]

There were few events that could not be gossiped over:

> 'Mr Collingwood,' returned Mrs Parkinson, 'it really is quite shocking. He dined with us the day before yesterday— cholera, I suppose—dreadful!' and Mrs Parkinson endeavoured to look quite overcome, but was not particularly successful. But Mrs Poggleton pretended nothing at all: she leant forward, held out her hand for the undertaker's circular, looked rather pleased than otherwise, and said, 'Dear me! If it is not the gentleman with that pretty carriage, I declare!' 'Small use to him a pretty carriage now,'

said Mrs Parkinson, 'the only carriage that he needs is a hearse.' 'Oh; but,' exclaimed Mrs Poggleton, with more eagerness than she had manifested throughout the conversation, 'I have been dying a long time for that carriage, and now I shall be able to get it. What a nice thing to be sure!'

Upon this Mrs Parkinson lifted up her hands, and pretended to be immeasurably shocked, muttering to herself, but quite loud enough for everybody to hear, that life was a span, and death hanging over us, and that the world might be destroyed tomorrow, for anything she knew to the contrary, with sundry other moral reflections of this kind, equally original, and expressive of virtuous emotion.[6]

Perhaps the main reason why so much gossiping took place was that, with the ready availability of cheap servants, British women, even the wives of common soldiers, had ample time on their hands. This was not always an advantage for the wives of ordinary soldiers, and an observer remarked that it was

only just [fair] to notice the temptations, restraints, and miseries, to which this class of women are subject, in a country so little calculated to cherish their better feelings, or to provide them with necessary occupation, or common comfort. Unable, from extreme heat, to move out of the little room allotted to them in the 'married men's quarters', during the day, and provided, for two rupees a month, with a Portuguese 'cook boy', who relieves them from the toil of domestic duties, the only resource of the soldiers' wives is in mischievous associations, discontented murmurings, and habits of dissipated indulgence. Strolling in the evenings through the dirty bazaars of a native town, probably under the auspices of an ayah [Indian nanny or nursery maid] who may have picked up a smattering of the English language, these unhappy women purchase liquor, to conciliate their careless husbands. On returning late to the barracks, the truant wife frequently finds her partner already in a state of intoxication.

Mutual recrimination follows, and then succeeds a scene for which we may well weep, that humanity has such.[7]

What happened in the families of the officer class, or among the administrators and merchants? For these better-off families, servants were even more affordable and thus more plentiful. Not that this meant they were always well treated. They were 'often visited with blows and such abuse as no respectable man will bear; very often too for no other fault than that of not understanding what the master has said, who has given his directions in some unintelligible stuff from ignorance of the language, that no one could understand'.[8]

Sadly, considerate behaviour by their British employers was not always understood by servants: 'One day I said to my ayah (a very elegant lady in white muslin), "Ayah, bring me a glass of toast-and-water if you please." She crept to the door and then came back again, looking extremely perplexed, and whined out, "What Mistress tell? I don't know." "I told you to bring me some toast-and-water." "Toast-water I know very well, but Mistress tell if you please; I don't know *if you please*."'[9]

While the growing legion of British women in India were busy with the rather inward-looking world of the European community, with servant problems, and bringing up small children in a difficult climate, their menfolk got on with the task of governing the Company's possessions. As commerce became a less important part of the Company's activities, and the ruling and taxing of Indian territory more significant, the administration and the army provided the twin pillars upon which British interests rested.

It was the administration that presented the fairer, more enlightened face of British rule. Recruits into the Civil Service had first to pass a fairly stiff entrance examination into the Company's college at Haileybury:

> Each candidate shall be examined in the four gospels of the Greek Testament, and shall not be deemed duly qualified for admission to Haileybury College, unless he be found to possess a competent knowledge thereof. . . . Nor unless he be able to render into English some portion of the works of one of the following Greek authors: Homer, Herodotus, Xenophon, Thucydides, Sophocles, and Euripides.
>
> Nor unless he can render into English some portion of the works of one of the following Latin authors: Livy, Terence, Cicero, Tacitus, Virgil, and Horace; and this part of the examination will include questions in ancient history, geography, and philosophy.
>
> Each candidate shall also be examined in modern history and geography, and in the elements of mathematical

science, including the common rules of arithmetic, vulgar
and decimal fractions, and the first four books of Euclid.
He shall also be examined in moral philosophy, and in the
evidences of the Christian religion as set forth in the works
of Paley.[10]

If he passed through Haileybury, the new recruit sailed
at his own expense round the Cape of Good Hope to one of
the three administrative 'Presidencies' of Bengal, Madras,
or Bombay. The cost of a cabin out could be £100, without
any furniture, a steep price for the early nineteenth century, even though administrators were generally well paid
on arrival. The voyage out was a tedious one and lasted
between three and four months. At least it got the new
man used to heat and boredom.

Recruits to the Company's army passed through the
military college at Addiscombe, before sailing for India.
The army in India numbered some 200,000 men by the
middle of the nineteenth century, the vast majority of
whom were sepoys (Indian foot soldiers); in normal times
there were perhaps 5,000 British personnel.

The East India Company's officers were often highly
prized as social 'lions' in India:

> In Europe there are separate classes of people who subsist
> by catering for the amusements of the higher classes of
> society, in theatres, operas, concerts, balls, etc., etc. But in
> India this duty devolves entirely upon the young civil and
> military officers of the government, and at large stations it

really is a very laborious one, which often takes up the whole of a young man's time. The ladies must have amusement; and the officers must find it for them, because there are no other persons to undertake the arduous duty. The consequence is that they often become entirely alienated from their men, and betray signs of the greatest impatience while they listen to the necessary reports of their native officers, as they come on or go off duty.[11]

Despite the heat and the dust, and the distance from home, routine military duties were scarcely exhausting:

Well, a black rascal makes an oration by my bed every morning about half an hour before daylight. I wake, and see him salaaming [bowing] with a cup of hot coffee in his hand. I sit on a chair and wash the teaspoon till the spoon is hot and the fluid cold, while he introduces me gradually into an ambush of pantaloons and wellingtons—if there is a parade. I am shut up in a red coat, and a glazed lid set upon my head, and thus, carefully packed, exhibit my reluctance to do what I am going to do—to wit, my duty—by riding a couple of hundred yards to the parade.[12]

For the other ranks, the barracks in India were as cheerless, noisy, and rough as any back in Britain:

The barracks were exceptionally noisy. The passage was sounding and reverberating, and each occupant of a quarter had much of the benefit of his neighbour's flute, fiddle or French horn, whether 'i' the vein' for harmony or not; shoe brushings, occasional yells of servants undergoing the discipline of fists or cane, jolly ensigns and cadets clattering up and down, cracking horsewhips [and] whistling. . . . On the ground might be seen a goodly display of trays, with egg shells, fish bones, rice, muffin, and other wrecks of breakfast; sweepers—certain degraded menials . . . squatting near and waiting for the said remnants; hookahs . . . in course of preparation for those who indulged in the luxury of smoking.[13]

One of the greatest of Victorian military men, Lord Roberts of Kandahar, looking back on his early Indian service after a distinguished career in the forces of the Empire, wrote in 1898: 'The men were crowded into small badly-ventilated buildings, and the sanitary arrangements were as deplorable as the state of the water supply. The only efficient scavengers were the huge birds of prey called adjutants, and so great was the dependence placed upon the exertions of these unclean creatures that the young cadets were warned that any injury done to them would be treated as gross misconduct.'[14]

Yet it was these badly educated, poorly paid, and harshly disciplined troops who, with their sepoy comrades, carried the power of the East India Company and Britain into the remote corners of the subcontinent. As for the overriding purpose of conquest and control, beyond the fundamental commercial and revenue advantages, there were increasingly sharp divisions of opinion.

One tricky issue was what was the essential aim of the British administration towards its millions of Indian subjects? Attitudes varied strikingly. One British memsahib said of the Indians: 'Thank goodness, I know nothing at all about them, nor I don't wish to. Really, I think the less one sees and knows of them the better.'[15] Although perhaps based on fear and thus a protective contempt of the 'other', this was a widespread, though hardly a benevolent, attitude.

Other members of the ruling British elite saw their role in India with more humility:

> The most important of the lessons we can derive from past experience is to be slow and cautious in every procedure which has a tendency to collision with the habits and prejudices of our native subjects. We may be compelled by the character of our government to frame some institutions, different from those we found established, but we should adopt all we can of the latter into our system. . . . Our internal government . . . should be administered on a principle of humility, not pride. We must divest our minds of all arrogant pretensions arising from the presumed superiority of our own knowledge, and seek the accomplishment of the great ends we have in view by the means which are best suited to the peculiar nature of the objects. . . .
>
> All that Government can do is, by maintaining the internal peace of the country, and by adapting its principles to the various feelings, habits, and character of its inhabitants, to give time for the slow and silent operation of the desired improvement, with a constant impression that every attempt to accelerate this end will be attended with the danger of its defeat.[16]

Despite these lofty sentiments, the period from 1815 to 1857 saw increasing conflict between the Company and various sections of Indian society. Even attempts at educational reform antagonized some of those who were supposed to benefit. Thomas Macaulay, the historian, was a member of the Governor General's Council in the early 1830s. In 1835 he put the case for the propagation of British education and culture in a famous government minute:

> To sum up what I have said: I think it is clear that we are free to employ our funds as we choose; that we ought to employ them in teaching what is best worth knowing; that English is better worth knowing than Sanskrit or Arabic; that the natives are desirous to be taught English, and are not desirous to be taught Sanskrit or Arabic; that neither as the languages of law, nor as the languages of religion, have the Sanskrit and Arabic any peculiar claim to our encouragement; that it is possible to make natives of this country thoroughly good English scholars, and that to this end our efforts ought to be directed.
>
> In one point I fully agree with the gentlemen to whose general views I am opposed. I feel, with them, that it is impossible for us, with our limited means, to attempt to educate the body of the people. We must at present do our best to form a class who may be interpreters between us and the millions whom we govern; a class of persons, Indian in blood and colour, but English in taste, in opinions, in morals, and in intellect. To that class we may leave it to refine the vernacular dialects of the country, to enrich those dialects with terms of science borrowed from the Western nomenclature, and to render them by degrees fit

vehicles for conveying knowledge to the great mass of the population.[17]

Although an increasing number of Indians took advantage of the new European education thus offered, others believed that the British were merely trying to train non-European servants of the East India Company and to degrade their own cultural traditions. 'The British Government', argued one Indian critic,

> professes to educate the Natives to an equality with Europeans, an object worthy of the age and of Britain. But if Englishmen, after educating the Natives to be their equals, continue to treat them as their inferiors—if they deny the stimulus to honourable ambition, and show the Natives that there is a barrier over which superior Native merit and ambition can never hope to pass . . . are they not in effect undoing all that they have done, unteaching the Native all that he has been taught, and pursuing a suicidal policy, which will inevitably array all the talent, honour and intelligence of the country ultimately in irreconcilable hostility to the ruling power.[18]

Controversies over educational issues, however, directly affected only a small number of Indians. The work of missionaries and evangelical Christians, on the other hand, was another matter. The missionary zeal that the authorities encouraged in the early 1800s aroused a much more generalized hostility. To many Indians it seemed as if the British were determinedly attacking the ancient religions of India.

These anxieties were compounded by the fact that a more self-confident company also came down hard on Indian customs that it considered uncivilized. Although this was an inevitable part of the 'imperial civilizing mission', its consequences were complex and potentially destabilizing, sometimes unexpectedly so.

In 1829 the practice of suttee (or sati) was declared illegal in Bengal, an example later followed in other British provinces. Suttee was the supposedly voluntary burning alive of Hindu widows on the funeral pyres of their dead husbands. British disapproval of such an apparently barbarous custom was understandable. In 1818 a police superintendent in lower Bengal wrote:

> There are very many reasons for thinking that such an event as a voluntary suttee rarely occurs. Few widows would think of sacrificing themselves unless overpowered by force or persuasion, very little of either being sufficient to overcome the physical or mental powers of the majority of Hindu females. A widow, who would turn with natural instinctive horror from the first hint of sharing her husband's pile, will be at length gradually brought to pronounce a reluctant consent because, distracted with grief at the event, without one friend to advise or protect her, she is little prepared to oppose the surrounding crowd of hungry Brahmins and interested relations. . . . In this state of confusion a few hours quickly pass, and the widow is burnt before she has had time to think of the subject.
>
> Should utter indifference for her husband, and superior sense, enable her to preserve her judgment, and to resist

the arguments of those about her, it will avail her little.
The people will not be disappointed of their show. . . . The
entire population of a village will turn out to assist in drag-
ging her to the bank of the river, and in keeping her on the
pile.[19]

Although Hindu reformers approved of the suppression of
suttee, millions more saw it as undue interference in a
custom sanctified by four millennia of practice.

Between 1829 and 1837 the Company also suppressed
thugee. The 'Thugs' were composed of bands of robbers
who strangled their victims as sacrifices to the goddess Kali.
They were described as 'the cunningest Robbers in the
World. . . . They use a certain slip with a running noose
which they can cast with so much slight about a Man's
Neck when they are within reach of him, that they never
fail; so that they strangle him in a trice.'

Another ubiquitous custom was female infanticide.
Throughout India, the killing of unwanted girl babies was
commonplace. With so many mouths to feed, poor families could not always afford to keep girl babies who would
need dowries when they came to be married—dowries that
could push the bride's family into chronic and disabling
indebtedness. But the practice was not only found in
impoverished families. For example, a landowner described
how when his daughter

> was born he was out in his fields . . . the females of the
> family put her into an earthen pot, buried her in the floor

of the apartment where her mother lay, and lit a fire over the grave. . . . He made all haste home as soon as he heard of the birth of a daughter, removed the fire and earth from the pot, and took out his child. She was still living, but two of her fingers which had not been sufficiently covered were a good deal burned. He had all possible care taken of her, and she still lives; and both he and his wife are very fond of her. . . .

He had given no orders to have her preserved, as his wife was confined sooner than he expected. But the family took it for granted that she was to be destroyed. . . . In running home to preserve her, he acted on the impulse of the moment. The practice of destroying female infants is so general among this tribe, that a family commonly destroys the daughter as soon as born, when the father is from home, and has given no special orders about it, taking it to be his wish as a matter of course.[20]

It was one of the great paradoxes of British rule in India that the Company, which seemed conservative and backward-looking to many British observers, seemed radical and reforming to Indian traditionalists when it attacked practices like these. The suspicion and resentments that were thus accumulating were bound ultimately to lead to a dramatic confrontation.

The confrontation was undoubtedly hastened by the controversial governor generalship of the energetic and confident Lord Dalhousie (1848–56). By 1856 large sections of Indian opinion had been antagonized. Dalhousie's policies, and his administration's apparently cavalier attitude towards Indian customs and sensibilities, caused wide-spread resentment.

Often it was the Victorian thrust for technological advance and 'improvement' that caused the problem. For instance, the rapid expansion of the railway system in British India seemed admirable and 'civilizing' to Europeans. Among devout Hindus, however, the introduction of the railways aroused fears that the caste system would be damaged by the physical contact inevitable on crowded trains.

Dalhousie had also annexed several Indian provinces between 1848 and 1856, some of them by reviving the controversial 'doctrine of lapse'—the convention whereby a local ruler without a legitimate heir stood to forfeit his province to the paramount power—now the Company. In 1856 Dalhousie annexed Avadh, the last great independent Muslim ruled state in North India. The pretext—internal disorder—was a reasonable one:

> The landowners keep the country in a perpetual state of disturbance, and render life, property and industry everywhere insecure. Whenever they quarrel with each other, or with the local authorities of the Government, from whatever cause, they take to indiscriminate plunder and murder over all lands not held by men of the same class. No road, town, village or hamlet is secure from their merciless attacks. Robbery and murder become their diversion, their sport, and they think no more of taking the lives of men, women and children who never offended them than those of deer and wild hog. They not only rob and murder, but

> seize, confine, and torture all whom they seize and suppose
> to have money or credit till they ransom themselves with
> all they have or can beg or borrow.[21]

It was more complicated than that. Significantly, Avadh lay between two of the major centres of British provincial power—Bengal and Punjab. It straddled the vital means of communication, notably the Grand Trunk Road from Calcutta to Delhi, as well as the Ganges and Jumna rivers. At the same time it was an obstacle to the construction of railway links driving westwards from Bengal. Forty per cent of the sepoys in the Bengal Army, the largest of the Company's three armies, however, were recruited from Avadh. The Avadh-born sepoys were bound to their place of origin by an intricate network of family and hierarchical relationships and obligations, so their pride was affronted by the abrupt removal of the ruler of the province. They were thus suddenly potential rebels.

The resentments caused by the annexation of Avadh were to mingle with many other discontents throughout British India. Moreover, the Company's armies, recruited to keep control of the subcontinent, now ironically provided ideal arenas within which barrack-room lawyers and assorted agitators could communicate very effectively with their fellows. Within a year of Dalhousie's departure for Britain, and public acclaim there, the great Mutiny or rebellion threatened to sweep away the very foundations of British power.

5

'The devil's wind': The Great Indian Uprising, or Mutiny, of 1857–1858

The terrifying Indian rebellion of 1857 caused considerable damage to Victorian self-esteem. It also struck a ferocious blow at European security by putting the lives of thousands of British men, women, and children at risk. Furthermore, it seemed to threaten comfortable British assumption that sound and efficient administration was enough to keep imperial subjects content, or at least passive.

The uprising went beyond the army and involved considerable numbers of Indian civilians, thus serving as a reminder that the great mass of Indian people could not be taken for granted as perpetually docile subjects. For a while British rule was effectively ended in a large area of northern India centring on the Gangetic plain. The onward march of British imperial and commercial control seemed to have faltered badly.

Why did this great rebellion happen in the first place? There is no doubt that the uprising of 1857 began as a mutiny in the Bengal Army, and was subsequently sustained by the action of other regiments in that force. The first violent protest took place at Meerut, thirty-six miles north-east of Delhi, on 10 May. There men of the Third Native Light Cavalry had been court-martialled for refusing to use the new greased cartridge that was being issued to units of the Bengal Army. As a result, eighty-five of the mutinous sepoys were sentenced by a court, composed of Indian officers, to ten years hard labour. Perhaps the fact that the mutineers were subsequently humiliated by their divisional commander, Major-General Hewitt, known as 'Bloody Bill', when on 9 May he had them paraded shackled with leg irons before their comrades in a ritual of public disgrace, aggravated the situation. In any event, that night the other sepoy regiments rose in rebellion, released the prisoners from jail, burnt down bungalows and offices, and killed any Europeans that fell into their hands. They then marched off, flags flying, towards Delhi.

The question is, what had finally pushed the sepoys at Meerut to the point of mutiny and rebellion? The controversy over the greased cartridges was undoubtedly the flash point. The East India Company had decided, from the early 1850s, to equip its sepoy regiments with the new

Enfield rifle in place of the smooth-bored 'Brown Bess' musket. As in so many other aspects of interaction between Britain and India, the new Western military technology seemed to strike at the heart of Indian tradition and faith. The rifled barrel of the new weapon required the cartridges to be greased so that the bullet that was placed in the base of each cartridge could be rammed home easily. Furthermore, the loading procedure for these new 'bored' rifles meant that the top of the cartridge had to be torn, or more probably—especially in the heat of action—bitten off, the gun powder poured down the rifle barrel, and finally the empty container with its bullet inside it rammed down the barrel.

Unfortunately rumours had been circulating since January 1857 that the great arsenal at Dum-Dum, near Calcutta, was coating the new-issue cartridges with pig and animal fat. To the Hindu the cow was a sacred animal; the Muslim believed that contact with the unclean pig would defile him. Amazingly the suspicions of the sepoys seemed to have been well founded, and provided a clear indication of the insensitivity of the British authorities towards Indian religious susceptibilities.

Hostile reactions to the new cartridges had first occurred in February 1857, affecting Indian troops at Barrackpur, close to Calcutta, and had later spread to a number of Bengal Army cantonments along the Ganges valley. Faced with mutinous regiments, some commanders took the sensible step of reassuring their troops that no attack on their religion was intended, while others tried by threats and bullying tactics to break the will of their sepoys. Indian regiments that seemed too unstable were disbanded, and on 21 April a mutinous sepoy at Barrackpur, Mangal Pandey, was court-martialled and hanged. By early May, there was widespread unrest amongst much of the Bengal Army.

If discontent had been confined simply to the controversy over the new cartridge, a general uprising might not have resulted. There were, however, other reasons why Indian troops in the service of the East India Company were discontented with their conditions. The fear that the Company was undermining their religion had precipitated earlier mutinies in 1806 and 1824, and as late as 1852 a regiment had refused to serve in Burma, since crossing the sea could have involved its Hindu troops in a loss of caste. By the mid-1850s the sepoys were being subjected to a process of military modernization and adjustment. There were rumours that the army would be disbanded now that Britain had completed its process of subcontinental conquest and pacification. In 1856 the General Service Enlistment Act stipulated that all new recruits should in future swear that they would cross the sea for military service, though this could involve Hindu troops in ritual pollution and had to be undertaken for no extra pay.

The inevitable stresses of barrack life and the demands of military routine and discipline could in themselves forment a spirit of resentment, especially if British officers were unable to maintain close and cordial relationships with their men. There is, in fact, a good deal of evidence to show that a breakdown in mutual esteem and goodwill had occurred between officers and sepoys well before the great uprising of 1857.

An Indian officer in the East India Company's service, Subedar Sita Ram, who later published a book entitled *From Sepoy to Subedar*, wrote tellingly of the immediate pre-Mutiny period: 'I always was good friends with the English soldiery and they formerly used to treat the sepoys with great kindness . . . these soldiers are of a different caste now—neither so fine nor so tall as they were; they seldom can speak one word of our language, except abuse.' A British observer, writing in the early months of the Mutiny in the North West Provinces, confirmed these impressions, saying of the British treatment of the sepoy: 'He is sworn at. He is treated roughly. He is spoken of as a "nigger". . . . The younger men seem to regard it as an excellent joke, and as evidence of spirit and as a praiseworthy sense of superiority over the sepoy to treat him as an inferior animal.'[1]

Inevitably the causes of the uprising went far deeper than military discontent. The territorial annexations and reforming policies of the East India Company had affronted many sections of Indian society in the half-century before the Mutiny. For the overwhelming majority of the Indian subjects of British rule, it was fundamentally irrelevant whether the Mughal Emperor, the Maratha Confederacy, or the East India Company ruled them; the perennial struggle for subsistence was the overriding preoccupation of peasant India, fatalistic and passive, not an armed rebellion against the paramount power.

From the summit of Indian society, however, things could look very different. As a result of the activities of the East India Company, the British had abruptly overthrown Indian rulers, had dispossessed landlords, and had seemed to encourage attacks on the indigenous religious and cultural order. The proselytizing of evangelical Christian missionaries, and the assault on local religious practices such as suttee, in conjunction with other social and economic reforms, could easily be perceived as part of the Company's insidious programme to subvert Indian traditions.

As we have seen, the governor generalship of Lord Dalhousie, from 1848 to 1856, intensified resentments that had been building up for many years. Dalhousie confidently asserted the paramountcy of the Company, thus also implying the superiority of British ways over Indian. His plans to improve road and rail communications were justified in terms of military security, but seemed to be further, perturbing, examples of change to Indian traditionalists. Finally, Dalhousie's unbridled policy of territorial annexation was bound to alienate local rulers and their followers.

Sepoys within the Bengal Army, in contrast to the rank-and-file soldiers of British armies recruited at home, were often from the higher sections of Indian society: Brahmins and Rajputs if they were Hindus, or members of good-class Muslim families if followers of Islam. On joining their regiments, moreover, they did not become mere faceless instruments of Company policy; they maintained their religion, their caste, and their family connections. Their continuing, complex links with their families had a double-edged significance: one was that they were especially sensitive to any fears or resentments that affected their families; the other was that they had an important status to maintain in the eyes of their relatives. Any apparent slight to their religion, any insult to their caste or standing, could result in rejection by family and friends, and loss of face

The local unrest emanating from the 1856 annexation of Avadh fed into other Indian resentments. In particular, the recent annexations of the Company had broken one of the cardinal rules of the maintenance of British power in India—that is, the policy of collaborating with powerful local elites. During his high-handed governor generalship, Dalhousie had dispossessed local rulers, either under the application of the 'doctrine of lapse', or for alleged misdemeanours, and Company economies had caused a cutback in the pensions normally paid in compensation to displaced princes. It is surely significant that two of the foremost princely supporters of the rebellion, the Nana Sahib in Avadh and the Rani of Jhansi, both felt aggrieved on these counts.

The uprising that began at Meerut in May 1857 took eighteen months to put down completely—in many ways this was a surprisingly long time. In 1857, however, there were only eleven British infantry regiments available for action, mainly because substantial numbers of troops were returning from the recent, triumphant war in Persia. As a result, several crucial strategic military and civil locations were without European troops, including the large arsenal in Allahabad, at the meeting point of the Ganges and Jumna, and Delhi, which was also an important military base as well as being the home of the last Mughal Emperor Bahadur Shah II. At the outset of the rebellion, therefore, the mutineers were easily able to take possession of strategic points and to seize a mass of arms and munitions.

The progress of the uprising was erratic and full of contradictions. One remarkable aspect was the failure of the rebellion to spread. The armies of Bombay and Madras remained loyal, and only a quarter of the sepoys in the Bengal Army joined the revolt. With the exception of the Nana Sahib and the Rani of Jhansi, the Indian princes gave unswerving support to the British. Recently conquered territories like the Punjab remained quiet, and troublesome border territories like Afghanistan and Nepal offered no assistance to the rebels. Indeed, Sikhs from the Punjab, and Gurkhas recruited in Nepal, played a considerable part in suppressing the Mutiny. No foreign power threatened to intervene, although it is difficult to see how they could have done, given the power of the Royal Navy and Russia's recent defeat in the Crimean War.

The mutineers themselves seemed to have lacked coherent leadership or any common plan. Some wished to restore the Mughal Emperor to his throne, but the old man refused to accommodate them. Others wished to restore those bits of the past that they particularly cherished. Often bands of mutineers roamed the countryside looting, and as a consequence antagonized the peasantry to whom they might otherwise have looked for support. Those peasant groups that did join the rebellion were soon cowed by the ferocity of the British and loyalist counter-attack. Despite the avowed intention of most of the mutineers to overthrow British rule, many regiments progressed through the countryside, their bands playing British marching tunes and their regimental flags flying proudly above them.

Despite the humiliations of the mutineers' early successes, the rebellion affronted British sensibilities in a number of dark and profoundly disturbing ways. To begin with, the assault of Indian rebels, particularly the mutinous sepoys of the Bengal Army, upon sections of the European civil and military population included violence directed at British women and children. The Kanpur (Cawnpore) massacre of captive British females and their offspring confirmed some of the worst fantasies of the European imperial imagination.

Just as in the uprisings of black slaves in the Caribbean and North America, the white, male response to the menacing, 'uppity nigger' of the Bengal Army was an explosive and lethal mixture of fear and loathing. At the heart of this uncompromising reaction was a horror of the sexual violation of white women by black men. The fact that the Indian rebels of 1857, overwhelmingly, it seems, did not rape their female captives did nothing to alter the conviction that an unspeakable violation had occurred.

The prospects facing the British families trapped in the besieged towns of Kanpur or Lucknow were undeniably grim. The best they could hope for was that the siege would be short, and that food and drink would last out. At worst, they would have to face defeat and, very probably, a cruel and savage death. The fate awaiting British women and children if the mutineers seized Lucknow was uncertain. There were fearful rumours of sepoy atrocities, of women raped, and babies tossed on bayonets for sport. In Lucknow one British man wrote:

> several of the men contemplated the destruction of their females if the enemy should overpower us. I was, during those terrible days, one evening taken aside by a military man, who was one of my garrison. He had, he told me, agreed with his wife that if the enemy should force his way in, he should destroy her. She had expressed herself

content to die by a pistol ball from his hand. He was, he told me, prepared, if I should fall, to do the same deed of despair to my own wife.[2]

Among those besieged at Lucknow were Katherine Bartrum, and her fifteen-month-old son, Bobbie. Katherine had been sent into the Residency at Lucknow, unwillingly leaving her husband, Captain Robert Bartrum, at an outstation. A group of loyal sepoys escorted Katherine and her son into Lucknow. She did not trust them: 'Sometimes they made our elephants stand whilst they lay upon the ground laughing and talking; but whenever I asked them for water for baby to drink, they would give it to me.'

Once safely inside the Residency of Lucknow, Katherine was 'fully occupied in nursing, and washing our clothes, together with cups and saucers, and fanning away the flies which have become a fearful nuisance'. When the children were asleep 'we used to gather round a chair, which formed our tea-table, sitting on the bedside, and drinking our tea (not the strongest in the world) by the light of a candle which was stuck in a bottle. . . . And then we talked together of bygone days, of happy homes in England where our childhood had been spent.'[3]

Eventually the forces of Generals Outram and Havelock fought their way into Lucknow. But they were not strong enough to break out again. Captain Bartrum was killed just as he was reaching the safety of the Residency. The widowed Katherine endured the double ordeal of grief, and a prolonged siege. She lacked soap, so 'we have to use the dhal [chick peas] by grinding it between two stones and making it into flour, and this is a good substitute for soap. But we have so little of it, that it is a question sometimes whether we shall use it to wash with, or to eat.'[4]

When Katherine finally left Lucknow in November 1857, she wrote:

> Heard that we are to leave Lucknow tomorrow night, with just what we can carry. Well! I can only carry my baby, and my worldly effects can be put into a very small compass, since they consist merely of a few old clothes. My heart fails me at the thought of the terrible march, with no one to look after me or care for me but God. I have lost my kind friend Dr Darby, who has been wounded; and they say he will not recover. He promised to take care of me on the journey to Calcutta, but now I am utterly friendless.[5]

She did reach Calcutta, but her child had been so weakened by his deprivations that he sickened and died. Katherine sailed for England, widowed and childless. Her experiences were not unusual in the unpredictable, terrifying, and chaotic disruptions caused by the Mutiny.

Although the Company's authority lapsed for a time in Delhi, Avadh, north-central India, and some of Bengal, two-thirds of the country remained uninvolved, even if sympathies were felt towards the rebels. When it came down to it, the Mutiny was small beer compared to the

Crimean War, which had ended in 1856, and the American Civil War that was to break out in 1861.

As the British troops fought their way into towns like Cawnpore, Lucknow, and Delhi, they carried out terrible reprisals. The atrocities of the sepoys were repaid in kind. Mutineers were given, at best, short military trials. Mostly they were shot down, bayoneted, or hanged—sometimes in pigs' skins to defile Muslims, or in cows' skins to mortify Hindus. In many cases, mutinous sepoys were tied to the mouths of cannons and blown into fragments of flesh and intestine.

General Neill, in Cawnpore, enforced a punishment that was extraordinarily sadistic, even as revenge for the massacred women and children:

> I wish to show the Natives of India that the punishment inflicted by us for such deeds will be the heaviest, the most revolting to their feelings and what they must ever remember. . . . The well [that had contained British bodies] will be filled up, and neatly and decently covered over to form their grave. . . . The house in which they were butchered, and which is stained with their blood, will not be washed or cleaned by their countrymen [but by] such of the miscreants as may hereafter be apprehended, who took an active part in the Mutiny, to be selected according to their rank, caste and degree of guilt. Each miscreant, after sentence of death is pronounced upon him, will be taken down to the house in question under a guard and will be forced into cleaning up a small portion of the blood-stains; the task will be made as revolting to his feelings as possible,

1. East India House, the Sale Room. The London Headquarters of the East India Company

2. Portrait of the Mughal Emperor Jahangir, who ruled during the early
   seventeenth century

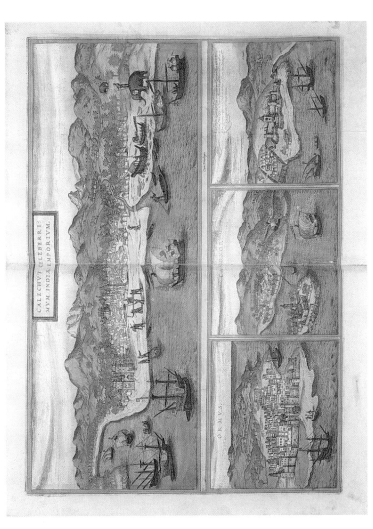

CALECHVT CELEBERRI
MVM INDIÆ EMPORIVM.

ORMVS.

3. Map of Calcutta before its development by the East India Company

A VIEW OF PART OF ST THOME STREET, FORT ST GEORGE.

4. View of St. Thome Street, Fort St George (later Madras) in the late eighteenth century

5. Mole Station, Bombay; Bombay became the ceremonial 'gateway to India' under the British

6. Lord Clive and family; Robert Clive led the British to success during the mid-eighteenth century

7. 'The young lady's toilet', 1842; Indian servants were cheap and plentiful

8. Sati: a Hindu widow burns to death on her husband's funeral pyre before the British outlawed the practice in 1829

PRIVATE FIRST BELOCH REGT.
AFGHAN.
BOONNEE MUSSULMAN.
SIND.
927-2.

9. A private from the First Beloch Regiment, recruited in Sind

10. Sikh troops in the East India Company's Armies; Sikhs were among the most loyal of sepoys

11. The Railways became the pride of British India, but their construction aroused fears that contributed to the great rebellion, or mutiny of 1857–8

12. British forces storm Delhi, during the repression of the 1857 rebellion

13. Aftermath of the Indian Mutiny 1857–58; bones of slaughtered rebels litter a
courtyard in Lucknow

THE ACCESSION OF THE QUEEN OF INDIA.

14. A Punch cartoon of 1858 celebrates the Crown taking control of British India after the 1857–8 rebellion

15. A dinner party at a British cantonment, 1860

16. Queen Victoria in 1890, attended by one of her favourite servants, the Indian Abdul Karim, 'the Munshi'

17. Transport for the rulers of India

18. Cricket teams, 1865. Indians developed a passion for this most English of games

19. A dandy, or sedan chair

20. Rudyard Kipling;
born in India and
the great poet
and story-teller
of the Raj

21. Hyderabad Contingent Polo Team in the early 1900s, with Indian and British players

and the Provost Marshal will use the lash in forcing any-
one objecting to complete his task. After properly cleaning
up his portion, the culprit is to be immediately hanged.[6]

Further south, the rebel town of Jhansi was ruthlessly
sacked by the victorious British forces:

> Fires were blazing everywhere, and although it was night I
> could see far enough. In the lanes and streets people were
> crying pitifully, hugging the corpses of their dear ones.
> Others were wandering, searching for food while the cattle
> were running mad with thirst. . . . How cruel and ruthless
> were these white soldiers, I thought; they were killing
> people for crimes they had not committed. . . .
>   Not only did the English soldiers kill those who hap-
> pened to come in their way, but they broke into houses
> and hunted out people hidden in barns, rafters and
> obscure, dark corners. They explored the inmost recesses
> of temples and filled them with dead bodies of priests and
> worshippers. They took the greatest toll in the weavers'
> locality, where they killed some women also. At the sight
> of white soldiers some people tried to hide in haystacks, in
> the courtyards, but the pitiless demons did not leave them
> alone there. They set the haystacks on fire and hundreds
> were burnt alive. . . . If anybody jumped into a well the
> European soldiers hauled him out and then killed him, or
> they would shoot him through the head as soon as he
> bobbed out of the water for breath.[7]

The suppression of the Mutiny became a bloody assize,
where the common British soldiers killed on the slightest
suspicion: 'I seed two Moors [Indians] talking in a cart.

Presently I heard one of 'em say "Cawnpore". I knowed what that meant. So I fetched Tom Walker, and he heard 'em say "Cawnpore", and he knowed what that meant. So we polished 'em both off.'[8]

The London *Times* was soon growling that 'this blind and indiscriminate exasperation is resolving itself into the mere hatred of a dark skin'. Generally, however, British opinion rejoiced in the overthrow of the mutineers. Citizens of good standing informed each other that: 'The Sepoys have taken to inflicting the most exquisite cruelties upon the Sikhs, and the Sikhs in return swear that they will stamp the Company's arms in red-hot [copper coins] over the body of every sepoy who comes their way.'[9]

The Victorian public was gorged on the horrors of the 1857 Indian uprising. Cartoons and drawings in newspapers and journals expressed a predictable sense of national outrage while at the same time titillating their readers' imaginations, with lurid, and generally irresponsible, images of mayhem. Indian troops were shown enthusiastically perpetrating atocities, and one print entitled 'English Homes in India, 1857' depicted a pair of dishevelled and blood-stained mutineers about to lay their reeking hands upon the heads of defenceless infants and upon the bosom of a breast-feeding British mother.

The 1857 revolt provoked other feelings of British outrage. Perhaps the most persistent of these, as well as the most unreasonable, was a sense of betrayal. The sepoys that rose in rebellion, the civilians that abetted and sometimes joined them, the few local princes who lent support to the uprising were all caricatured and vilified as ungrateful and treacherous wretches, violently rejecting the manifold benefits bestowed by Britain's civilizing mission in the subcontinent.

It is not difficult to see why this response took place. The rebellion seemed to be a fundamental reaction against the prevailing Victorian belief in progress. A nation that was not merely the world's leading industrial and commercial power, but one that was apparently extending to the Indian subcontinent the same concrete reforms that were paving and lighting the streets of Britain's cities, believed that it had ample cause for self-congratulation.

As Queen Victoria's reign unfolded, the idea of Empire was increasingly a source of pride to British people, and the alleged achievements of British rule were generally taken for granted. The conquest, control, and reordering of indigenous societies in India and elsewhere also enabled the dispossessed of Victorian Britain to luxuriate in an unaccustomed feeling of superiority and virtue. Rage at the rebels' delinquency included even those at the bottom of the domestic social structure, as illustrated in the cartoon of a begrimed dustman and sweep discussing 'this 'ere Hingia bisinis' and agreeing that 'it's just wot yer might expeck from sich a parcel o' dirty black hignorant scoundrels as them'.

All this helps explains why the Victorians were so determined to describe the uprising of 1857 as 'the Indian Mutiny'. By defining it in this fashion it was possible to contain the events within a military framework, and so to deny the wider, infinitely more threatening ramifications. The whole affair could be dismissed as the work of groups of malcontent Indian mercenaries, their benighted religious prejudices enflamed by the agitation of barrack-room lawyers, rather like the Chartists at home were caricatured as irresponsibly befuddling the minds of normally docile and god-fearing workingmen and women.

It is also significant that Mangal Pandey, the sepoy who first mutinied and who was subsequently hanged at Barrackpur in April 1857, was rumoured to have been stimulated to carry out his attack on his British officers by the use of drugs. In these ways the 'unpleasantness' of 1857 could be written off as the results of overindulgence in hashish or as the ill-informed responses of peasants in uniforms to unscrupulous agitation. So successful was this bid to rewrite the agenda for the rebellion of 1857 that it is only very recently that British historians and writers assessing the event have chosen words other than 'mutiny' to describe the uprising, or have acknowledged the part played by civilian rebels.

As a consequence, many bruised and bitter feelings were left by the Mutiny. Deep-seated prejudices, which had already been much in evidence before 1857, were confirmed and strengthened. The gulf that had already opened between the two races widened to almost unbridgeable proportions. One of the major casualties was trust. It now became more difficult for British officers, merchants, or even administrators to see many Indians in a favourable light. In a matter of moments, apparently steadfast soldiers and loyal servants had been transformed into murderous, raping fiends. The almost universal approval in Britain of the often ferocious measures taken to put down the uprising of 1857 were part of a national mood of retribution and despair. As a result, among the many casualties of the rebellion, even if temporarily, were some of the more liberal assumptions concerning Indian progress and possible political developments.

The rebellion of 1857 provided the opportunity to restructure Britain's relationship with India. The East India Company was the main casualty of the uprising. Continuing the process of creeping state control, the 1858 Government of India Act swept away the power of the Company, which was assumed by the Crown. This at least brought theory into line with practice. The Company continued as a trading concern, but its great days were over. The Governor General was given the title of Viceroy by Royal Proclamation, but carried out the same duties. In order to focus its authority in London, the British government established a Secretary of State for India and a council of fifteen to advise him.

The creation of a Secretary of State for India, responsible to Parliament and advised by the India Council, was not all plain sailing. In its early years, the India Council consisted of ex-servants of the Company and thus tended to be conservative in its policies. The Secretary of State could, if he wished, ignore its recommendations and base his authority on Parliament.

Parliament's supervision could be fully affective only if MPs made it so. Indian affairs were remote from the interest of most Members of Parliament, and the average voter had only a hazy idea of the wherabouts and identity of India. Notoriously, the annual debate on the Indian budget sent MPs packing. As a result, the Secretary of State could often operate as he and the Cabinet thought fit. Even given a masterful Secretary of State, and a compliant Parliament, however, there was still the matter of overseeing and, if necessary, controlling the Viceroy. This powerful stand-in for the monarch was, however, 5,000 miles away, and not until the introduction of the telegraph in the 1880s could the process be anything but a lengthy and erratic process of communication.

There was an attempt to extend the scope of Indian government. The Central Legislative Council was expanded in 1861 by the addition of several non-official members, of whom two were Indians. This was, however, an almost worthless reform. The Legislative Council had hardly any legislative functions, and no power at all over the Viceroy's

Executive Council, which effectively acted as a British India's Cabinet. The two Indian non-officials were safe loyalists, not difficult or seditious politicians. The Viceroy's Council, moreover, was devoid of any democratic element, and it was the Viceroy's Council that ruled India. Finally, the Viceroy could veto any legislation passed in any council.

One other administrative reform was to have great significance for future development. This was the restoration of legislative functions to the councils of Bombay and Madras, and the establishment of legislative councils for Bengal, the Punjab, and the North West Provinces. Here again, the power was more illusory than real, though the councils could conceivably be, and indeed later were, utilized as vehicles for democratic experiment and progress.

Inevitably, the army was reconstructed after the Mutiny. All its troops were placed under the Crown. There was an attempt to increase the proportion of British soldiers, and initially a refusal to let Indian troops handle artillery. Since, however, Indian soldiers continued to outnumber British troops by two to one, the authorities tried to recruit 'reliable' men. As a result, the Indian army came to rely heavily on Sikhs, Gurkhas, and the frontier tribes of the north-west—who were Muslim.

One of the unexpected results of the crushing of the rebellion was the strengthening of conservatism within the subcontinent; as a result, orthodox Hinduism experienced a revival. Prior to 1857 reformist elements had been in the ascendant, but subsequent reaction tended to promote and sanctify the more obscure and traditionalist qualities of Hinduism as a protection against the inroads of 'corrupting' and 'dangerous' British ideas and influence.

Another deeply conservative element was reinforced by the uprising. The Indian princes had displayed almost unanimous loyalty during the rebellion. They now reaped their reward. Grateful for their stalwart support, the British decided to maintain them in place. As a consequence, the princely states were now safe from encroachment as long as they accepted British overlordship and advice.

Another bonus for the princes, and indeed for all conservative local elements, was the new caution exercised by Britain over the process of reform. Fearful to set in motion an Indian reaction similar to the one that had precipitated the great uprising of 1857, the government sought, wherever possible, to avoid drastic political and social change.

For the half century after the Mutiny, British rule in India was based upon conservatism tempered by pragmatism. As a result, it pursued a policy of containment and cautious development. It was not a state of affairs that could be maintained for ever.

6

Lords of All they Surveyed?
The Raj at its Zenith,
1858–1905

After the Mutiny, the British in India began the construction of a complex, multilayered, but fundamentally conservative, system of government. It was much easier, now that the Crown rather than the East India Company controlled India, to impose the policies and standards of the British government. As a consequence, the Indian Civil Service became an efficient, and on the whole fair, means of administering India. At the pinnacle of the administrative system was the Viceroy, who usually held office for four or five years. Under him there were the governors of the different provinces like Madras, Bombay, or the Punjab. Under the governors were the civil servants, law officers, police chiefs, and various other ranks.

For the thousands of British living in and working in India, whether permanently or on a tour of duty, life after the great uprising was a strange mixture of insecurity and unbounded confidence. The Mutiny had further widened the gulf between the races that had existed before 1857, with British women in particular becoming more fearful of a situation where, according to legend, fantasy, and gossip, one's long-serving Indian cook or gardener might at any moment become a raging atavistic beast intent on rape and bloodshed. On the other hand, the comprehensive crushing of the uprising seemed to confirm Britain's quasi-divine right to rule the subcontinent with a firm though kindly intent for the foreseeable future.

Nowhere was British self-confidence more clearly demonstrated than in the reordering of the central and local administration of India. Here the show not merely went on, but went on with more self-assertive splendour and ceremonial than previously. It was as if, having suffered the near catastrophe of the great uprising, the British were determined to demonstrate at every turn that they were indisputably in charge and likely to remain so for as long as either ruled or rulers could imagine.

Naturally, it was not quite as simple as that. Despite the pomp and power of the job, for instance, most Viceroys were not politicians of the first rank; rather they tended to be recruited from the ranks of politicians who had never quite made it at home, or who needed to be put out to grass somewhere far away; would-be Prime Ministers preferred to stay close to the seat of government at Westminster, patrolling the corridors of power rather than struggling with the often intractable problems of a poverty-stricken, sweltering subcontinent.

Once appointed, the Viceroy could act the part of a reformer, or of a conservative, during his period of office. Between 1858 and 1905, however, it would be fair to say that only two Viceroys tried to introduce important new measures: Lord Ripon (1880–4), a Viceroy appointed by a Liberal government; and Lord Curzon (1898–1905), who was appointed by a Unionist-Conservative government. As we have seen, the main reason why few reforms were made during these years was that the British feared that they would build up resentments similar to those that had caused the Indian Mutiny. This meant that a Viceroy had to be particularly forceful and resilient to push through reforms of any substance.

By the end of the Victorian era in 1901, the Viceroy had become one of the most powerful rulers in the world, as powerful in his own way as the Emperor of China. He seemed to possess unbridled power, although he could, in theory, be at any time recalled by the British government. He ruled over some 300 million subjects. At his disposal was one of the finest armies in the world, the Indian Army. Both the Indian Army and the Indian Civil Service were paid for out of taxes gathered in India. In this way, the

Indian people paid for the forces that kept them as obedient subjects and India as part of the British Empire.

India was, in many ways, the most important component part of the Victorian Empire. On average, nineteen per cent of British exports went to India, and hundreds of millions of pounds sterling were invested there. The Raj was thought to be a superb example of the incorruptible administration of a subject people by an imperial power. Thus, for economic reasons, as well as for reasons of prestige, India was described as the 'brightest jewel in the imperial Crown'. Few foreigners observing the spread and might of the Empire in India could doubt that Britain was the greatest power in the world.

As if to rub the point home, in 1877 Queen Victoria was proclaimed Empress of India. This was the brainchild of Benjamin Disraeli (1804–81)—the Conservative Prime Minister from 1874 to 1880. Always aware of the power of image and propaganda (not least for himself), Disraeli believed that, if his government gave Queen Victoria the new title, it would make the Indian princes, rulers of one-third of India, even more loyal in their support of the Raj.

Despite her glittering title of Queen-Empress, Queen Victoria never once visited India. Indeed, she visited none of her major possessions, preferring the royal retreats of Balmoral and the Isle of Wight to far-flung colonies. She was, however, proclaimed Empress with great pomp and ceremony. The heads of the Indian Civil Service, the

Indian princes, and thousands of troops attended the celebrations. Not all the ceremonial went as smoothly as clockwork.

The Indian princes brought their own troops and military bands: 'One venerable gentleman . . . had a man grinding God Save the Queen on a hand organ, when we entered his tent. [Another] had a band of bagpipes, and gave us God Bless the Prince of Wales, played by pipers as black as soot, but with pink leggings on their knees to make them like their Highland originals.'[1] When the new Empress was proclaimed, brass bands and trumpeters heralded the event as the Viceroy read out the proclamation. The massed infantry then fired their rifles in the air: 'This was splendidly executed and with excellent effect, for it made the rajahs jump, and raised quite a stampede among the elephants, who "skedaddled" in all directions, and killed a few natives.'[2]

In order both to gratify and to group them, the Indian princes were each given new coats of arms, which were displayed on banners of heavy Chinese satin. Again, there were unforeseen difficulties and the Viceroy, the reactionary Conservative, Lord Lytton (1876–80), wrote to Queen Victoria telling her that the fault of the banners was 'that the brass poles, which are elaborately worked, make them so heavy that it requires the united efforts of two stalwart Highlanders to carry one of them. . . . Consequently, the native chiefs who have received them will, in future processions, be obliged, I anticipate, to hoist them on the backs of elephants.'[3]

Queen Victoria's proclamation as Empress was, however, fundamentally a spectacular and symbolic ceremony amid the never-ending, complex, and serious business of ruling a teeming and overwhelmingly backward sub-continent. The everyday preoccupation of the Raj was to enforce law and order, to try to improve public health and public education, to advance irrigation schemes, and to deal with huge problems like famine control and agricultural efficiency.

Inevitably, given the scale and depth of the tasks that faced it, the British administration could make only relatively slow progress. Even if the Raj had spent far more money on the problems it faced, progress would have remained slow. It is worth remembering that, even back home in the United Kingdom, social and political reforms only gradually and painfully emerged for much of the nineteenth century.

Sometimes the British administration in India sought to play down the problems. When Florence Nightingale (1820–1910), the redoubtable nursing and medical reformer, surveyed health conditions in the Indian Army in 1863, she wrote, when questioned about drainage, that 'the army in India was like the London woman who replied, "No, thank God, we have none of them foul, stinking things here". . . . Bombay, it is true, has a better water supply; but it has no drainage. Calcutta is being drained but it has no water supply. Two of the seats of Government have thus each one half of a sanitary improvement, which halves ought never to be separated. Madras has neither. . . . At Agra it is a proof of respectability to have cess-pools. The inhabitants (152,000) generally resort to fields.'[4]

Crises, when they came to India, were often on a vast, almost unmanageable scale. For example, the country was frequently gripped by terrible famines, affecting tens of millions of people. Clearly the Raj had to provide famine relief. Many Victorians, however, believed that charity would undermine self-help, and thus did not want to give too generously. Typically, the Famine Commission, set up in 1880, stated that relief should be given so as 'not to check the growth of thrift and self-reliance among the people. . . . The great object of saving life and giving protection from extreme suffering may not only be as well secure but in fact will be far better secured, if proper care be taken to prevent the abuse and demoralization which all experience shows to be the consequence of ill-directed and excessive distribution of charitable relief.'[5]

In 1900 Lord Curzon, from the comfort of the viceroyalty, argued that: 'In my judgement any government which imperilled the financial position of India in the interests of a prodigal philanthropy would be open to serious criticism. But any government which, by indiscriminate almsgiving, weakened the fibre and demoralized the self-reliance of the population would be guilty of a public crime.'[6]

After the disastrous famine of 1899–1900, Curzon, who had at least introduced a new famine policy in 1901, was hopeful about the future:

> We may compete and struggle with Nature, we may prepare for her worst assaults, and we may reduce her violence when delivered. Some day perhaps when our railway system has overspread the entire Indian continent, when water storage and irrigation are even further developed, when we have raised the general level of social comfort and prosperity, and when advancing civilization has diffused the lessons of thrift in domestic expenditure and greater self-denial and control, we shall obtain the mastery. But that will not be yet. In the meantime the duty of the government has been to profit to the full by the lessons of the latest calamity and to take such precautionary steps over the whole field of possible action as to prepare ourselves to combat the next.[7]

The Raj also consistently attempted to improve India's agricultural system. This was literally a matter of life and death, since over 70 per cent of the population were completely dependent upon agriculture. To begin to make headway against deep-rooted traditions and practices was not easy.

Lord Mayo (Viceroy 1869–72) summed up the problem in a dispatch:

For generations to come the progress of India in wealth and civilization must be directly dependent on her progress in agriculture. . . . There is perhaps no country in the world in which the State has so immediate and direct an interest in agriculture. The Government of India is not only a Government but the chief landlord. The land revenue is derived from that portion of the rent which belongs to the State, and not to individual proprietors. Throughout the greater part of India, every measure for the improvement of the land enhances the value of the property of the State. The duties which in England are performed by a good landlord fall in India in a great measure upon the Government. Speaking generally, the only Indian landlord who can command the requisite capital and knowledge is the State.[8]

Interestingly, Mayo was anxious not to cause a hostile reaction against his proposed agricultural reforms:

In connexion with agriculture we must be careful of two things. First, we must not ostentatiously tell native husbandmen to do things which they have been doing for centuries. Second, we must not tell them to do things which they can't do, and have no means of doing. In either case they will laugh at us, and they will learn to disregard really useful advice when it is given.[9]

The Viceroy went on to admit that he did not know 'what is precisely meant by ammoniac manure. If it means guano, superphosphate, or any other artificial product of that kind, we might as well ask the people of India to manure their ground with champagne.'

Under British rule, Indian industry developed rapidly from the 1880s, so much so that by 1914 India was among the top fourteen most industrialized nations—a remarkable fact, even though its place was near the bottom of the table. Indigenous enterprise and capital played a major part in this process, beginning in 1887 when a modern cotton mill was opened at Nagpur by the Parsee J. N. Tata. The Tata family were later to build up the Indian iron and steel industry, and to establish a commercial presence that is still much in evidence in India in the early twenty-first century.

Until 1911 expansion was mainly limited to the cotton and jute industries, as a government report of 1902–3 pointed out:

Nothing illustrates better the present state of industrial development in India than the fact that after the cotton and jute industries . . . there was only one of the manufacturing industries . . . namely the iron and brass foundries, in which as many as twenty thousand persons are returned as having been employed during the year. In the preparation of agricultural staples for the market, employment is found for larger numbers; indigo factories . . . employed over 81,000 workers; cotton ginning, cleaning and pressing mills over 65,000; jute presses, 22,000. But of manufacturing industries, properly so-called . . . the most important, after cotton and jute mills, are the iron and brass foundries (20,674), silk filatures (10,652), tanneries (8,626), and others of still less importance.[10]

From 1858 to 1905, therefore, the Raj could claim some credit for economic, legal, and educational improvements. A more difficult question remained, however: what was the long-term aim of the British in India? Would not the emergence of a class of highly educated Indians mean that one day, maybe sooner rather than later, these men would call for a greater say in the government of their own country? Might not India demand independence in due course?

The Victorians could not seriously consider the collapse of the Raj, which, at least until 1905, looked so secure. In 1901 Lord Curzon put the point dramatically when he stated, 'As long as we rule India we are the greatest power in the world. If we lose it, we shall drop straightaway to a third-rate power.'[11]

Traditionally, and in response to the first, modest stirrings of Indian nationalism from the 1880s, the British in India were at pains to stress that they were engaged on a noble mission of ruling a lesser people for their own good. In 1903 Curzon, who believed this more passionately than most of his contemporaries, said:

> If I thought it were all for nothing, and that you and I, Englishmen, Scotchmen and Irishmen in this country, were simply writing inscriptions on the sand to be washed out by the next tide; if I felt that we were not working here for the good of India in obedience to a higher law and a nobler aim, then I would see the link that holds England

and India together severed without a sigh. But it is because I believe in the future of this country and the capacity of our own race to guide it to goals that it has never hitherto attained, that I keep courage and press forward.[12]

Not that the task of ruling India was always a noble and high-minded matter. A lot of what the British saw was squalid and depressing. Admittedly, some British residents found a certain 'backward charm' about the impoverished villagers, too concerned with survival to be a political nuisance:

> I know the malgoozar [headman] of every village, and many of the inhabitants of the knots of hovels scattered over the land. Perhaps 'hovel' is too harsh a name for those snug and sunny mud abodes, with their thatched roofs covered with melons. . . . What though the mistress of the house labours daily as a coolie for the Biblical price of a sparrow, and carries grain, earth, wood or water on her head, with a high-kilted sari [long dress] and inimitable grace, and the master spends his time in sitting aloft in a . . . basket, raised on a stick in a . . . field, clapping with a wooden clapper. . . . In short, acting as a scarecrow? Still, when the stone-carrying and parrot scaring are over for the day, many merry talkative parties may be met, returning joyously to bake the immortal chupattie [a sort of pancake] and to feast.[13]

Whether attempts to improve the lot of the great mass of Indian peasantry would make the British more secure and better liked as rulers was uncertain. Lord Lytton put his finger on this quandary in 1877 when he said:

> I am convinced that the fundamental mistake of able and experienced Indian officials is a belief that we can hold India securely by what they call good government; that is to say, by improving the condition of the peasant, strictly administering justice, spending immense sums on irrigation works, etc. Politically speaking, the Indian peasantry is an inert mass. If it ever moves at all, it will move in obedience, not to its British benefactors, but to its native chiefs and princes, however tyrannical they may be.[14]

Overall, however, the Indian peasantry were unlikely to cause serious trouble for the Raj. The most potentially difficult Indians in the late-Victorian era were the educated 'babus'. These men were the products of the system of English education in India, and may well have graduated from Calcutta or Bombay universities. Inevitably, they held a very difficult position in society. In effect, they had been transformed into brown Englishmen, but in practice were denied the chance to get the best administrative jobs in their own country.

As a consequence, they often used their wasted talents in criticizing the Raj. Lord Lytton wrote scornfully of them in 1877: 'The only political representatives of native opinion are the Babus, whom we have educated to write semi-seditious articles in the native Press, and who really represent nothing but the social anomaly of their own position.'[15]

Lord Mayo was scornful and resentful of the part that he perceived the babus generally playing:

> In Bengal, we are educating in English a few hundred Babus at great expense to the State. Many of them are well able to pay for themselves and have no other object in learning than to qualify for government employ. In the meantime we have done nothing towards extending knowledge to the million. The Babus will never do it. The more education you give them the more they will keep to themselves and make their increased knowledge a means of tyranny.[16]

For many British in India, and at home, the prospect of admitting the babus, or indeed any Indians, to a real share of power under the Raj was unthinkable. John Strachey, a member of the Viceroy's Council in the 1860s and 1870s, thought that power could not be entrusted 'to the hands of Natives, on the assumption that they will always be faithful and strong supporters of our government. In this there is nothing offensive or disparaging to the Natives of India. It simply means that we are foreigners, and that, not only in our own interests, but because it is our highest duty towards India itself, we intend to maintain our dominion.'[17]

Predictably, Curzon was much more outspoken, unreasonably so. In 1901 he stated that the strength of his position as Viceroy lay in 'the extraordinary inferiority in character, honesty and capacity of the Indians. It is often said why not make some prominent native a member of the Viceroy's Executive Council? The answer is that in the whole continent there is not an Indian fit for the post.'[18]

Many British liberals and radicals saw things differently. In an article written in 1877, the great Liberal leader William Ewart Gladstone looked more sympathetically at Indian hopes and aspirations:

> The question who shall have supreme rule in India is, by the laws of right, an Indian question; and those laws of right are from day to day growing into laws of fact. Our title to be there depends upon a first condition, that our being there is profitable to the Indian nations; and on a second condition, that we can make them see and understand it to be profitable. . . . It is high time that these truths pass from the chill elevation of political philosophy into the warmth of contact with daily life; that they take their place in the working rules, and that they limit the daily practice, of the agents of our power. . . . For unless they do, we shall not be prepared to meet an inevitable future. We shall not be able to confront the growth of the Indian mind under the very active processes of education which we have ourselves introduced.[19]

The more enlightened attitudes of people like Gladstone were often fiercely resented by members of the British community in India. Many of them felt that Indian advancement threatened their high-salaried jobs and their social position, quite apart from the foundations of the Empire in India.

In 1883 the bitter controversy over the Ilbert Bill showed the deep prejudices of many of the British in India. The Bill, named after the legal member of the Viceroy's

Executive Council, proposed that, since many Indians were becoming qualified to act as magistrates, they should be allowed to practise, and to try Europeans brought before them. Many of the British community were incensed at this proposal. One of them, Mrs Annette Beveridge, insisted that the Bill would subject 'civilized women [i.e. Englishwomen] to the jurisdiction of men who have done little or nothing to redeem the women of their own race, and whose social ideas are still on the outer verge of civilization'.

The editor of the *Friend of India* weighed in: 'Would you like to live in a country where at any moment your wife would be liable to be sentenced on a false charge, the magistrate being a copper-coloured Pagan?'[20] The hysterical reaction to the Ilbert Bill worked. The measure was amended so that Europeans would be tried only by an all-white jury.

Despite its high-minded official aspirations, British rule was based on the fundamental belief in the superiority of Europeans over 'natives'. Blatant racial prejudice was commonplace in British India. Some of its manifestations were supposedly humorous, like the newspaper advertisement that read: 'WANTED Sweepers, Punkah Coolies, and Bhisties [water carriers] for the residents of Saidpur. None but educated Bengali Babus who have passed the University Entrance Examination need apply. Ex-Deputy Magistrates (Bengali) preferred.'[21]

Sometimes satirical British writers aimed at bigger and more sensitive targets, like the anonymous author of a poem that openly mocked the Muslims:

> O grim and ghastly Mussulman [Muslim]
> Why art thou wailing so?
> Is there a pain within thy brain
> Or in thy little toe?
> The twilight shades are shutting fast
> The golden gates of day,
> Then shut up, too, your hullabaloo –
> Or what's the matter, say?
>
> That stern and sombre Mussulman,
> He heeded not my speech
> But raised again his howl of pain,—
> A most unearthly screech!
> 'He dies!'– I thought, and forthwith rushed
> To aid the wretched man,
> When, with a shout, he yell'd—'Get out!
> I'm singing the Koran!'[22]

All too frequently, the British might simply kick Indians out of their way or cuff their servants about the ears. Wilfrid Blunt, while in India, objected to a British passenger on a train in a station threatening some nearby Indians with a stick. The passenger was indignant 'at my venturing to call him to account. It was his affair not mine. Who was I that I should interpose myself between an Englishman and his natural right?'[23] To his credit, Blunt eventually got the irate man to apologize, but such contrition was not always forthcoming.

On the other hand, the British observer, writer, or parliamentarian who visited India and dared to criticize the Raj was likely to be even more unpopular than the awkward, 'jumped-up' babus. It was assumed, of course, that these visitors never understood India at all: 'Mr Cox, the member of Parliament—perhaps you may remember him?' 'A little red-haired fellow, was he? Who wrote a book about India on the back of his two-monthly return ticket?'[24]

Kipling also wrote scathingly of 'Pagett, M.P.':

Pagett M.P. was a liar, and a fluent liar therewith,
He spoke of the heat of India as 'The Asian Solar Myth',
Came on a four months' visit to 'study the East' in
     November,
And I got him to make an agreement vowing to stay till
     September.

April began with the punkah, coolies, and prickly heat,
Pagett was dear to mosquitoes, sandflies found him a
     treat.
He grew speckled and lumpy—hammered, I grieve to say,
Aryan brothers who fanned him, in an illiberal way.

July was a trifle unhealthy,—Pagett was ill with fear,
Called it the 'Cholera Morbus', hinted that life was dear.
He babbled of 'Eastern exile', and mentioned his home
     with tears
But I hadn't seen my children for close upon seven years.

We reached a hundred and twenty once in the Court at
  noon,
(I've mentioned that Pagett was portly) Pagett went off in
  a swoon.
That was the end to the business. Pagett, the perjured,
  fled
With a practical, working knowledge of 'Solar Myths' in
  his head.

And I laughed as I drove from the station, but the mirth
  died out on my lips
As I thought of the fools like Pagett who write of their
  'Eastern trips',
And the sneers of the travelled idiots who duly misgovern
  the land,
And I prayed to the Lord to deliver another one into my
  hand.[25]

The summer heat that has so badly affected 'Pagett
M.P.' proved equally troublesome to those who upheld the
Raj. 'Prickly heat', for instance, was described as 'a sort of
rash which breaks out on you, and, as its name infers, is
prickly in its nature. I can only compare it to lying in a
state of nudity on a horse hair sofa, rather worn, and with
the prickles of the horse hair very much exposed, and with
other horse hair sofas above you, and all around, tucking
you in. Sitting on thorns would be agreeable by compari-
son, the infliction in that case being local.'[26]

Despite Noel Coward's later lampoon of 'Mad Dogs
and Englishmen', it was in practice best for Europeans to

shelter from the sun between midday and two o'clock in the afternoon: 'The, white sunlight lies upon the roads in so palpable a heat that it might be peeled off: the bare blinding walls, surcharged with heat, refuse to soak in any more. . . . In the dusty hollows of the roadside the pariah dogs lie sweltering in dry heat. Beneath the trees sit the crows, their beaks agape. The buffaloes are wallowing in the shrunken mud-holes, but not a human being is abroad of his own will.'27

When the weather became cooler, or in the evenings, it was possible to enjoy a promenade in a respectable part of town, to listen to the military music being played in the bandstand, to admire the red poinsettias (a tropical flower): 'One could go to friends for dinner, or perhaps to an official reception. When the rains came, the garden would sprout overnight, the roof might leak . . . and cockroaches and snakes invade the verandah.'

Despite the drenching monsoon rains, it was the Indian heat that was generally considered worse and more dangerous. In the hot season, those families who could afford it went to the hill stations, many of which became similar to holiday resorts. Here the air was crisp and cool, and diseases like cholera were kept at bay. The most famous hill station was Simla, where the Viceroy and his retinue came to escape from Calcutta's feverish heat. Simla, and other hill stations, soon acquired the reputation for a vigorous social life, romance, and adulterous liaisons.

Before all this could be experienced, however, the women and children had to travel from the plains to the hills. This is how it was proposed to transport a typical family consisting of a mother, three or four children, and a nurse or ayah:

1st camel load: Two large trunks and two smaller ones—with clothing.

2nd camel load: One large trunk containing children's clothing, plate chest, three bags, and one bonnet-box.

3rd camel load: Three boxes of books, one box containing folding chairs, light tin box with clothing.

4th camel load: Four cases of stores, four cane chairs, saddlestand, mackintosh sheets.

5th camel load: One chest of drawers, two iron cots, tea table, pans for washing up.

5th camel load: Second chest of drawers, screen, lamps, lanterns, hanging wardrobes.

7th camel load: Two boxes containing house linen, two casks containing ornaments, ice-pails, door mats.

8th camel load: Three casks of crockery, another cask containing ornaments, filter, pardah (purdah) bamboos, tennis poles.

9th camel load: Hot case, milk safe, baby's tub and stand, sewing-machine, fender and irons, water cans, pitchers.

10th camel load: Three boxes containing saddlery, kitchen utensils, carpets.

11th camel load: Two boxes containing drawing room sundries, servants' coats, iron bath, cheval glass, plate basket.

Or the above articles could be loaded on four country carts, each with three or four bullocks for the up hill journey. . . . A piano, where carts can be used, requires a cart to itself, and should be swung to avoid being injured by jolting. If the road is only a camel road, the piano must be carried by coolies, of whom fourteen or sixteen will be needed. . . . When a march is made by stages, and one's own cows accompany, these latter should start, after being milked, the night before the family.[28]

When they could not holiday with their families, the men carried on the work of the Raj. Often newly recruited Indian civil servants, fresh from Britain, had enormous and lonely responsibilities. This description of the life of a young judge in a remote district is not untypical:

Here is Tom, in his thirty-first year, in charge of a population as numerous as that of England in the reign of Elizabeth. His Burghley [Elizabeth's chief adviser] is a joint magistrate of eight-and-twenty, and his Walsingham [another of the Queen's councillors] an assistant magistrate who took his degree at Christ Church within the last fifteen months. These, with two or three superintendents of police, and last, but by no means least, a judge who in rank and amount of salary stands to Tom in the position which the Lord Chancellor holds to the Prime Minister, are the only English officials in a province one hundred and twenty miles by seventy. . . . he rises at daybreak, and goes straight from his bed to the saddle. Then off he gallops across fields bright with dew to visit the scene of the late robbery; or to see with his own eyes whether the crops of the zemindar [landlord] who is so unpunctual with his assessment have really failed; or to watch with fond parental care the progress of his pet embankment.[29]

The Indian Army, too, had its essential, and sometimes rough part to play in the service of the Raj. Disease and drink and debauchery were all too often the lot of the common soldier, but more often it was just a hot, hard slog:

> We're marchin' on relief over Inja's coral strand,
> Eight 'undred fighting Englishmen, the Colonel, and the
>   Band;
> Ho! Get away you bullock man, you've 'eard the bugle
>   blowed,
> There's a regiment a-coming down the Grand Trunk
>   Road;
> With its best foot first and the road a-sliding past,
> An' every bloomin' campin'-ground exactly like the last.[30]

British rule seemed better established during the latter part of Queen Victoria's reign than ever before. The Indian Civil Service and the Indian Army remained the twin pillars that upheld the stately structure of the Raj. As the twentieth century opened, they seemed part of a permanent and almost divine order. As it happened, the Raj was less than fifty years away from total collapse and disintegration.

7

The Beginning of the End?
Reform and Conflict,
1905–1919

T he years following Curzon's resignation in 1905
saw a dramatic turning of the tide in the relationship between rulers and ruled in India. This
was partly to do with the impact of seismic, global events
like the First World War. But increasingly powerfully
organized internal Indian protest, as well as the advent of
a Liberal government in Britain in December 1905, also
played a major part in creating the changed atmosphere.

To a significant extent, the alteration in mood derived
from the failure of the self-imposed, highly publicized,
reforming, though reactionary, agenda of Lord Curzon,
Viceroy from 1898 to 1905. When Lord Curzon resigned in
1905, he had not succeeded in his self-appointed task of
binding the Indian people even more closely to Britain.

Indeed his viceroyalty had been marked by highly charged conflict and controversy, much of it either between himself and the British government, or with senior administrators in India.

Curzon had wanted to bring strategically important border states like Afghanistan and Tibet under the control of the Government of India. His aggressive policies led to clashes with the Unionist and Conservative Prime Minister, A. J. Balfour (1902–5), particularly since the British administration wanted to leave these countries alone rather than risk conflict with Imperial Russia as Britain moved towards the 1904 diplomatic entente with France, Russia's close ally.

He had also quarrelled publicly and spectacularly with the Indian Commander-in-Chief, Field Marshal Kitchener (1902–6), over who controlled Indian defence and military spending—the Viceroy's Executive Council or the Commander-in-Chief. Indeed, it had been this embarrassing battle between two self-regarding and primadonna-like men that had led to Curzon offering Balfour his resignation in 1905, only to be mortified when it was promptly accepted.

Curzon had also clashed with many senior Indian civil servants and with some of the commanders of the best regiments in India. After one titanic conflict with a crack cavalry unit, the Ninth Lancers, over the beating to death of an Indian cook in 1902, Curzon sent off the whole regiment, aristocratic officers and all, to a posting in the deeply unpopular colony of Aden. When he finally left for home in 1905, it was claimed that there was hardly any Indian official of any standing whom he had not personally insulted and confronted—from the iconic, brooding, world-famous Kitchener to relatively junior members of the Indian Civil Service. In a way, therefore, much of his reforming zeal—the reform of agricultural and irrigation policy, the preservation of India's ancient monuments, the desire to encourage Indian trade and commerce—had been wasted in high-profile and enervating disputes.

Worse still, before he left he had sanctioned the partition of the ancient province of Bengal. This move, which was supposed to make the administration of Bengal simpler and more effective, aroused violent hostility among the Bengali people. The outcry in Bengal, which contained some of the best-educated and most politically aware citizens in all India—the home in fact of the 'Bengali babu'—was taken up by nationalist leaders throughout the subcontinent.

This was doubly unfortunate for the Raj, as by the early twentieth century organized political movements were challenging the smooth running of the administration, and were soon to threaten the very existence of the Raj. The Indian National Congress, founded in 1885 with enthusiastic British support, had, after twenty years, outlived its original role as a harmless talking shop. Curzon's high-handed and abrasive viceroyalty helped to transform Congress into a far more radical and effective organization. As we have seen, Curzon had hoped, through demonstrating the impartiality and effectiveness of British rule, to bind India permanently to the Raj. Ironically, his partition of Bengal, and the bitter controversy that followed, did much to revitalize Congress. Curzon, typically, had dismissed the Congress in 1900 as 'tottering to its fall'. But he left India with Congress more active and effective than at any time in its history.

The foundation of the Muslim League in 1906 was another warning that the post-Mutiny settlement, based upon administrative conservatism and minor concessions to Indian constitutional progress (as expressed in the 1892 Indian Councils Act), had broken down. When Gandhi returned to his home country in 1915, the scattered and varied forces of Indian nationalism were to gain their most skilful, shrewd, and populist leader to date.

Faced with these new pressures, the British tried to rally the loyal and conservative elements in the country: the princes, men like the Maharajahs of Bikaner and Hyderabad, who had so much to lose if the Raj collapsed, and who ruled a third of the country; the deeply entrenched landlord class, and some of the rapidly rising indigenous industrialist and entrepreneurial class—such as the Tata family.

If the 'haves' of Indian society were generally biddable in the sense that their prosperity and status made them unlikely to be nationalist revolutionaries, the Indian masses, the swarming, huddled 'have-nots', were also tractable and docile overall. Of course, local disputes, often over rents and conditions of service to landlords, could erupt swiftly and violently, but they remained essentially local rather than national disturbances. While the Indian nationalist movements remained low key and dominated by English-speaking politicians in well-cut suits, the peasant masses were even less likely to identify with the various issues raised at meetings of Congress or the Muslim League.

Despite all this, the strength of the Indian reaction to the 1905 partition of Bengal, and the 1908 split between Congress 'moderates' and 'extremists', also encouraged the Liberal government in Britain to introduce the Morley–Minto Reforms of 1908–09. The 1909 Indian Councils Act modestly extended the franchise, but quite substantially increased the numbers of elected and nominated Indians on the provincial and central legislative councils of the Raj. In a way, the reforms were a confidence trick. The British, by holding out the prospect of progress, at some time to be decided by themselves, towards responsible government, were undoubtedly hoping to contain and defuse the forces of Indian nationalism. Thus the extension of democratic institutions was used as a means of shoring up the fundamentally autocratic British Raj.

The ambiguous nature of the reforms of 1908 and 1909 was demonstrated by the correspondence between the Indian Secretary of State, Morley, and the Viceroy, Lord Minto, over which Indian should be nominated to sit on the Viceroy's Executive Council. The key appointment eventually went to S. P. Sinha, whom Minto preferred to the other potential appointee on the grounds that 'Sinha is comparatively white, whilst Mookerjee is as black as my hat!'[1]

If so crucial an appointment could be made, at least in part, on the grounds of acceptable skin colour, what hope was there for the many well-educated Indians of participating in the administration of their own country? Although the Indian Civil Service was theoretically open to Indian competition, the fact that the entrance examinations were held in the United Kingdom, and the weight of official disapproval at their advancement, ensured that only a handful of Indians had been appointed to the ICS by 1914.

The Morley–Minto Reforms produced a storm of criticism from the British community in India, and from conservative opinion at home. King Edward VII and the Prince of Wales (the future George V) were hostile. So were much of the press, and the Conservative Party. Arthur Balfour, the Leader of the Conservative Opposition, spoke against giving Indians a majority on the Legislative Councils in 1909:

> British administration, good or bad, lacking or not lacking sympathy with native feelings in all directions, is at all

events an honest administration sincerely desirous of pro-
tecting the poor and the masses of the community by stop-
ping corruption and oppression, which are too common
in all countries, and which are the special and poisonous
growth of Oriental despotism. Such a government [i.e. the
Raj] you do not want to control by these . . . majorities,
because to control them in that way prevents them carrying out their duties impartially.[2]

Indeed, British hostility to the 'educated native'
increased rather than decreased as the twentieth century
began. This was in direct ratio to the rate of Indian reform.
If more Indians were now aspiring to share in the administration of the country, then British reactionaries were more
likely to ridicule and to diminish them, and so to try to
contain them. The 'jumped-up Bengali babu' had been an
object of ridicule and contempt during the second half of
the nineteenth century. So was 'the copper-coloured pagan'
so strenuously denounced in the row over the Ilbert Bill,
with its proposal to allow Indians to practise as magistrates,
and even to try Europeans. As Indians gradually began to
avail themselves of the limited but developing opportunities
of gaining a university education within the subcontinent,
reactionary British wits took pleasure in joking about a new
Indian qualification: 'B.A. (failed) Calcutta'. In all these
ways, some covert, some open, but all pernicious, the spirit
of Macaulay's great Indian education reforms of the 1830s
was subverted by the growing need to keep India, with its

expanding economy and its supplementary army, safely within the Empire.

The Morley–Minto Reforms did not, as the pessimists forecast, bring about a collapse of the Indian Empire. Indeed, during the First World War (1914–18) India was a pillar of strength in the Allied cause. Over two million men were recruited. Indians fought in all the major theatres of the war. They died in their tens of thousands for a King-Emperor that hardly any had seen and for a country that very few had visited. They also fought with courage and loyalty in the bloody and incompetently led invasion of Mesopotamia—the notorious 'Mess-pot' campaign—in parts of German Africa, and especially on the Western Front, where recent research shows that they were too often put into more hopeless and hazardous positions than European troops.

The slaughter on the Western Front was so appalling, and the letters home of those able to write so disturbing, that men of the 5th Light Infantry, stationed at Singapore, mutinied when it was rumoured they were about to embark for France. Several officers were murdered, and gangs of mutineers killed several Europeans in Singapore in acts of random violence. In the ensuing panic, a British woman wrote: 'The Indian Mutiny flashed into my mind; also that we had no white troops.'[3]

Although the Singapore mutiny was crushed and thirty-seven of the ringleaders publicly shot, far more difficult to contain were the worries of devout Muslim troops, who were encouraged by their mullahs to object to the Allied assault on Turkey—the homeland of the Otto-man Emperor, the Caliph. The resulting Khilafat agitation spread beyond the army and for a while posed a serious threat to political stability in India.

Yet, despite all this, the Indian Army stayed over-whelmingly 'true to its salt'. In part to reward this invalu-able loyalty, and partly from a commitment to gradual political devolution, the British government decided to acknowledge what they saw as India's 'maturing' status and value within the Empire. As a consequence, in 1917 India was invited by the Prime Minister, David Lloyd George, to attend the Imperial War Conference held in London as a full member. This meant that some Indians represented India, together with their British colleagues, at these crucial deliberations to discuss the planning and running of the war. In this regard, India was now being treated as a near equal to the established Dominions of Australia, Canada, New Zealand, and South Africa. This high level of involvement was carried into the peace nego-tiations of 1918–19, when India was granted its own delega-tion at the proceedings and signed the resulting peace treaties in its own right.

Equally significant was the 1917 visit to India of the Indian Secretary of State, Edwin Montagu. As a result of his talks and meetings, Montagu made a significant pronouncement on the constitutional and political aims of British rule in the subcontinent. The 1917 Montagu Declaration stated that Britain's constitutional objectives were 'the increasing association of Indians in every branch of the administration and the gradual development of self-governing institutions with a view to the progressive realisation of responsible government in India as part of the British Empire'.[4]

Though a touch obscure to the Indian man or woman in the street or the bazaar, this was a vital statement of British policy. The crucial phrase was 'responsible government', which meant, within the context of past imperial evolution, the granting of a Westminster-type constitution with the executive responsible to a fully representative parliamentary assembly.

The central question for Indian nationalists, however, was 'when'? Although the commitment was undoubtedly serious, did it depend for its implementation upon continuing Indian 'good behaviour'; or was it simply an attempt to keep India 'on side' and loyal for the duration of an increasingly costly and unpopular war? Reform, and the promise of more to come, was especially useful as Indian Army casualties mounted (over 62,000 died in the conflict), as prices rose sharply in the bazaars and rents on the land, while there were unexpected food shortages, and while the Raj imposed heavy wartime restrictions upon the civil rights of Indians to dissent, criticize, and object to the war.

To add to their troubles, the British faced an even more potentially threatening challenge with the return to his native land of the British-educated barrister Mohandas Karamchand Gandhi, following his remarkable success in mobilizing local Indian political action against the white supremacist regime in South Africa. There Gandhi had developed a new technique of confrontation, *satyagraha*, or 'the strength of truth', whereby the weak could confront the strong in a non-violent way and thus attempt to win them over through example, restraint, and the power of superior moral character.

Although the British rulers of India were slow to recognize the fact, *satyagraha* had the potential dramatically to change the interaction between the Raj and its subjects, chiefly through its capacity to mobilize and empower the Indian masses to a hitherto unimaginable degree.

Although Gandhi did not unleash *satyagraha* upon the British authorities on a national scale until 1919, he achieved some remarkable local successes during 1917 and 1918 at Champaran, Kheda, and Ahmedabad. The post-war period was to see an exceptional escalation in the confrontation between the power of the Raj and the demands of Indian nationalism.

8

Gandhi and the Fightback of Indian Nationalism, 1919–1939

G andhi's arrival in India shortly after the outbreak of the First World War was to transform the nature of the increasingly tense and bitter struggle between the forces of Indian nationalism and the entrenched power of the British Raj. Though first seen by both the British and his fellow countrymen as a quirky, bemusing, and lightweight figure, Gandhi was to confound both friend and foe with the potency and impact of his political and personal philosophy.

Having spent over twenty years in South Africa, where he had developed the tactics of *satyagraha* and given the white minority government a good deal of trouble, Gandhi decided to return to India and to rediscover the land of his birth. Arriving early in 1915, Gandhi had at first seemed very much the odd man out among the Euro-peanized, highly educated leaders of India's nationalist movements.

Fellow Indians were puzzled. V. S. S. Sastri wrote: 'Queer food he eats; only fruit and nuts. No salt: milk-ghee etc being animal products avoided religiously. No fire should be necessary in the making of food, fire being unnatural. . . . The odd thing is he was dressed quite like a *bania* [a member of the trading and shop-keeping caste]: no one could mark the slightest difference.'[1] A leading newspaper, the *Madras Mail*, reported that:

> Mr. Gandhi does not lay so much store by agitation for obtaining concessions from the Government as by work-ing for the moral, material and economic regeneration of his countrymen, for he is of the opinion that once people make themselves fit by their character and capacity, the grant of privileges will follow as a matter of course—in fact, there will be no need for people to ask for the con-cessions, and what is granted will be no concessions, for people will have grown into them.[2]

To many among India's educated elite, Gandhi seemed to represent a rejection of progress. There was indeed a lot of evidence to support this impression. Gandhi's criticisms of Western education, which he now argued was a system designed to enslave and corrupt India, his opposition to the assimilation of Western scientific techniques, his advo-cacy and promotion of cottage industry, and his preference for the *ashram*, or religious retreat, to the factory or the college, all seemed steps backwards not forwards.

To many these views seemed dangerous obstacles to progress and reform, not least because large numbers of the Indian elite had eagerly appropriated the language, education, culture, and style of their foreign rulers. Indeed, one of Gandhi's chief mentors on his return to India, the moderate nationalist leader and academic Professor Gokhale, believed that 'the greatest work of Western education in the present state of India is . . . the liberation of the Indian mind from the thralldom of old-world ideas and the assimilation of all that is highest and best in the life and thought of the West'.

The editor of the *Indian Social Reformer*, K. Natrajan, sprang to the defence of Western civilization in the face of Gandhi's determined, calm, and rational attacks, acknowledging: 'You may not agree with us that Western Civilisation, taken as a whole, tends more strongly to justice for all than any other Civilisation. . . . Where we find, to our great regret, that we cannot follow you, is in your generalisation against the modern civilisation as such.'[3]

On Gokhale's advice, Gandhi spent much of the two years after his return to India travelling round the subcontinent, getting once more to know the homeland from which he had been away for so long. During 1917, however, he was persuaded to put his philosophy of *satyagraha*, tempered in the heat of South Africa's racial confrontations, into action in three local disputes. Although there were inevitably some inconsistencies in effectiveness and results, the *satyagraha* campaigns at Champaran, Kheda, and Ahmedabad during 1917 and 1918 made their mark. They were especially powerful in the propaganda war between rulers and ruled, since they each centred on Gandhi's capacity to mobilize and inspire ordinary Indians to take extraordinary measures, whether the indigo-growers of Champaran or the textile mill-workers of Ahmedabad. Above all, these three confrontations demonstrated to nationalist leaders and to the British administration the potential of the new Gandhian politics of passive civil disobedience and non-violent confrontation.

Why was *satyagraha* potentially so powerful a weapon? To begin with, it offered no violent physical challenge to the Raj. This was prudent, for the British Raj, with its patient construction of alliances with local collaborationist elites and groups, the playing-off of one section of Indian society against another, and the sheer scale of its military organization and commitment, could simply not be defeated by unarmed, even if revolutionary, civilians. Also *satyagraha*, practised on a nationwide scale, promised to involve literally millions of ordinary Indian people in a series of peaceful demonstrations that could eventually undermine the Raj's authority and the British administration's will to rule. Finally, owing mainly to the simplicity and quasi-religious qualities associated with *satyagraha*,

Indian resistance to British rule could become for the first time a mass movement, not the preserve of a Western-educated elite wearing suits, waistcoats, and ties and making speeches in English to audiences who could not always understand them.

Gandhi, who had abandoned his Western style of dressing as early as 1906 in South Africa, now became, through his prominence in India, one of the most daunting, charismatic, and at the same time paradoxical opponents of British imperialism. Shortly after his return in 1915, the British authorities, mindful of his subtle and unexpected successes in South Africa, and anxious to keep India as loyal as possible in wartime, had urgently commissioned a Bombay police report on him. After some investigation, the police inquiry concluded reassuringly that Gandhi was 'not a Bolshevik' but instead was undoubtedly some sort of 'psychological case'.

It is easy to see why so superficial a judgement could have been made. Gandhi's renunciation of the material world, and of most earthly, physical pleasures, was incomprehensible to many Indians let alone Westerners. Many British conveniently concluded that he was simply a wily, and almost certainly hypocritical, political tactician. For many others who observed him, whether Indians or Westerners, he had a particularly charismatic personality.

The British academic, socialist, and political activist Harold Laski wrote, after meeting him: 'It was fascinating to see Gandhi at work and try and penetrate his secret. It comes, I think, from what the Quakers call the inner light—the power of internal self-confidence which, having established its principles, is completely impervious to reason. . . . But the drama of this wizened little man with the whole power of the empire against him is a terrific spectacle. The basis of it all is, I think, the power of an ascetic over Eastern minds who resent the feeling of inferiority they have had for 150 years.'[4]

During 1919, Gandhi ceased to be a peripheral, even ludicrous, figure on the margins of nationalist politics, and within a few months had established himself, often against fierce opposition, as an all-Indian leader of considerable weight. This sea change was the result of his leadership of the nationalist movement, mostly through the agency of the Congress Party, during the Rowlatt *satyagraha* in 1919, which attempted to mobilize India's millions in a peaceful protest—involving prayer, fasting, and the refusal to work— that threatened to shake the foundations of the Raj.

The crisis arose because at the end of the First World War the Raj decided to pass legislation, embodied in the two Rowlatt Acts, that extended into peacetime the restrictive legislation of the wartime period. As a result, individual and group political and civil rights—such as free speech and the right to assembly—were to be severely restricted. Inevitably, Indian nationalists saw this as a gross affront and a serious threat to the effectiveness of their campaigning.

The strength of Gandhi and other nationalist leaders' rejection of the restrictive legislation contained in the Rowlatt Acts also sprang from the apparent inconsistencies in British policy towards India. As we have seen, the Montagu Declaration of 1917 had promised the introduction of a significant measure of responsible government, thus seeming to prove that the Raj was prepared to enter into a new and more intimate relationship with its Indian subjects, favouring cooperation over control and the devolution of political power over autocracy.

Nationalists were convinced that the Rowlatt legislation showed the real face of the Raj. Gandhi denounced the proposals as 'evidence of a determined policy of repression' and argued that Indians could not 'render peaceful obedience to the laws of a power that is capable of such a piece of devilish legislation'.

Worse was to follow with the Amritsar Massacre in April 1919, a tragedy that sprang partly from the success of the Rowlatt *satyagraha*. The British policy of combining coercion with kindness was not, of course, unique to the Indian situation in the aftermath of the First World War. Ireland, as so often in the past, was undergoing a very similar experience, and nationalist movements throughout the Empire were to become familiar with the iron fist within the silken glove.

The iron fist was tragically and violently in evidence in April 1919. On 13 April, Indian Army troops, led by

Brigadier-General Dyer, opened fire on a crowd of peaceful demonstrators in Amritsar, the holy city of the Sikhs in the Punjab. Dyer, who was a notoriously rigid and controlled personality, had calculated, apparently to the last bullet, how long the Gurkha and Baluchi troops under his command should sustain their fire.

The demonstrators, trapped within a walled yet open area, the Jallianwallabagh, and with the gates locked against their escape on British orders, were a predominantly Sikh crowd numbering roughly 10,000. They were subjected to one of the most brutal episodes in the history of the Raj. By the time Brigadier-General Dyer had ordered his troops to cease firing, nearly 400 Indians lay dead and more than 1,000 had been wounded.

The Amritsar Massacre was one of the great tragedies of British rule in India, and a public-relations disaster of grotesque proportions. The cold-blooded killings, and the public floggings and humiliations imposed upon Indians in the locality under martial law between 15 April and 9 June, prompted shocked reactions within the Empire and beyond.

A Commission of Inquiry, including an Indian member, reprimanded Dyer for his actions at Amritsar, and revealed that he had neither warned the demonstrators that they must disperse nor made any attempt to offer medical assistance to the wounded—insisting that they were free to apply to him for help. Despite this, no legal action was taken against him. Eventually Dyer was forced to take early retirement on half pay, although he went on to receive his army pension. The Commission did, however, condemn the public floggings of Indians for such offences as 'the contravention of the curfew order, failure to *salaam* [bow] to a commissioned officer, for disrespect to a European, for taking a commandeered car without leave, or refusal to sell milk, and for similar contraventions'. Interestingly in the aftermath of the Russian Revolution, the inquiry found no evidence of the alleged conspiracy to subvert law and order by 'Bolsheviks and Egyptians'.

Enraged and bewildered, Indian nationalist leaders were quick to condemn the atrocity. Gandhi announced that any cooperation with this 'satanic regime' was now impossible. The internationally acclaimed writer Rabindranath Tagore, angered by the substantial vote in the British House of Lords against Dyer's forcible retirement on half pay, wrote that 'no outrage, however monstrous, committed against us by the agents of their government can arouse feelings of indignation in the hearts of those from whom our governors are chosen'. He also complained that 'the enormity of the measures taken . . . had, with a rude shock, revealed to our minds the helplessness of our position as British subjects in India'. The young Jawaharlal Nehru, who had been educated at Harrow and Cambridge and was destined to be the first Prime Minister of an independent India, was shocked by 'this cold-blooded approval of the deed', which he found 'absolutely immoral, indecent; to use public school language, it was the height of bad form'.[5]

Among those who upheld and supported the Raj, however, the reaction was mixed. For many of the British living and serving in India, the firm hand showed at Amritsar was welcomed. One woman, the writer Maud Diver, wrote: 'Organised revolt is amenable only to the ultimate argument of force. Nothing, now, would serve but strong action and the compelling power of martial law. . . . At Amritsar strong action had already been taken. . . . The sobering effect of it spread in widening circles, bringing relief to thousands of both races.'[6]

When Dyer had ordered the public flogging of arrested rioters in Amritsar, some British onlookers had shouted: 'Strike hard, strike more!' A local commander in Delhi applauded Dyer's action, and described demonstrators there as 'the scum of Delhi', adding 'if they got more firing so much the better. It would have done them a world of good . . . as force is the only thing that an Asiatic has any respect for.'[7]

For years representatives of the British in India had called for tough measures against nationalist agitation, especially acts of violence: 'The wholesale arrest of the acknowledged terrorists in a city or district coupled with an intimation that at any repetition of the offence ten of them would be shot for every life sacrificed, would soon put down the practice of throwing bombs'.[8] Some British even claimed that large numbers of Indians were as relieved as themselves at Dyer's actions:

> No more trouble here or at Amritsar. . . . Martial law arrangements are being carried through to admiration . . . and in no time the poor deluded beggars in the city were shouting—'Martial law *ki jai*!' [long live martial law!]—as fervently as ever they shouted for Gandhi and Co. One of my fellows said to me; 'Our people don't understand this new talk of *Committee ki raj* [government by Committee]. . . . Too many orders make confusion. But they understand *Hukm ki raj* [government by order]. In fact, it's the general opinion that prompt action in the Punjab has fairly well steadied India—for the present at least.'[9]

Naturally there were British critics of the Massacre. Edwin Montagu, the reforming Secretary of State for India, expressed his displeasure only to be denounced by reactionaries as nothing better than 'a Bolshevik Pasha dealing out revolutionary generalities with the insolence of a tyrant on the divan'. Montagu's Under-Secretary at the India Office, the Indian peer Lord Sinha, reminded the House of Lords of the outrage generated among his countrymen at the Massacre and at the racial humiliations subsequently inflicted upon them. Even Winston Churchill, though privately approving Dyer's decision to 'teach a lesson', disapproved of his repeated assertion that he wished he had killed more demonstrators.

The causes of the Amritsar Massacre and the mixed responses to it tell us a great deal about the relationship between the rulers and the ruled in post-First World War India. The atrocity was a response—admittedly a bloody, shameful, and irresponsible one—to one of the most widespread and effective demonstrations against British rule since the Mutiny of 1857. During the Rowlatt *satyagraha*, very large numbers of Hindus and Muslims had protested in a variety of ways, some of them unexpected, against the Raj.

Already jittery as a result of the admittedly patchy success of the *satyagraha*, the British authorities were further provoked at the demonstrations in Amritsar, which had led to a series of violent incidents on 10 April, during which four Europeans had been killed and one female missionary physically assaulted. This chiefly explains the ferocity of the military response. Indeed, in General Dyer's cold-blooded and ruthless massacre of unarmed and peacefully demonstrating men, women, and children may be seen yet another example of the European male's tendency to violent overreaction in response to a physical threat to a white female.

It was also worrying for the Raj that the Punjab, particularly its large towns like Amritsar, had responded well to the call for nationwide demonstrations against British rule. The province had a particular significance in the history of the British in India: it was not only one of the main granaries of India, but it also provided a disproportionally large number of troops, both Sikhs and Muslims, for the Indian Army, as well as many members of the police force. Widespread demonstrations in the Punjab, therefore, were likely to provoke excessive anxiety within British ranks. Above all, there was the growing conviction among British administrators and residents in India that Gandhi's apparent triumph in tempting the Congress movement and other nationalist groups down the new path of *satyagraha* could strike a deadly blow at the heart of the Raj and hasten the end of British rule.

For Indian nationalists, on the other hand, the Rowlatt legislation and the Amritsar Massacre seemed simply to be offensive evidence of British hypocrisy and oppression.

It is easy to see why British policy in India seemed so full of contradictions. The truth was that, on the one hand, Britain wanted to hang on to a possession that was still of enormous, though declining, economic value, and that had great symbolic significance, while, on the other, it wished to be seen as facilitating an orderly process of liberal, constitutional devolution. It was a matter of having one's cake and eating it too.

In economic terms, the continuing, though falling value of the Indian market to the British economy made it impossible abruptly to hand over full independence to the Indian people and walk away. Between the two world wars,

India remained the symbolic centrepiece of the imperial structure, despite the fact that the percentage of British trade with the subcontinent fell quite significantly; for example, the net balance of trade in manufactures tumbled from a surplus £75,000,000 in 1924 to £22,700,000 in 1937.

As for the symbolic significance of ruling India, for a whole variety of reasons, some of which were paradoxical, complex, and instinctive, few of those prominent in British public life would have dissented from the view, first expressed by Lord Curzon in 1901, that the loss of India would mean that Britain would 'drop straight away to a third-rate power'. The end of Empire thus seemed to be inextricably bound up with the fate of the British rule in India. Interestingly, even Hitler believed that the British Raj both signified Britain's global status and was an admirable example of an Aryan civilizing mission.

In the inter-war period, however, it was no longer possible to sustain British control on the basis of the earlier self-confident and paternalistic imperialism epitomized by the viceroyalty of Curzon. British policy-makers attempted to grapple with the new situation by doling out enough constitutional concessions to satisfy Indian nationalist aspirations, while retaining India as a central and intrinsic part of the imperial system. It was a balancing act that could not be sustained for ever.

It is significant that the future of British rule in India was one of the most fiercely contested issues of the inter-war period. Perhaps inevitably, many Conservative MPs were far more concerned about Indian issues in the late 1920s and early 1930s than they were about unemployment. Literally millions of words were spoken and written on the subject. Even before he became Prime Minister for the second time in 1935, the Conservative Stanley Baldwin demonstrated an almost Gladstonian sense of mission on the subject, and committed his party to a process of substantial Indian reform.

The passions generated over India almost destroyed the political career of Winston Churchill, who resigned the Tory whip over Indian reforms, not as is commonly supposed over the issue of rearmament and opposition to the rise of fascism. He vehemently opposed the 1935 Government of India Bill and, as a member of the India Defence League, poured scorn on Gandhi: 'It is . . . nauseating to see Mr Gandhi, a seditious Middle Temple lawyer, now posing as a fakir of a type well known in the East, striding half-naked up the steps of the Viceregal palace . . . to parley on equal terms with the representative of the King-Emperor.' It is worth noting that, apart from Churchill, many contemporary political observers saw India as 'perhaps the central issue in parliamentary life'.[10]

It is thus understandable that Indian nationalists accused the British government of hypocrisy—though confusion over aims played a part too. It is evident that, at least within the Conservative Party—which after all dominated nearly every House of Commons between 1918 and 1945—there were elements that fought a persistent and relatively successful campaign against the granting of full independence to India. Even the two minority Labour administrations of the inter-war period, either through their weak parliamentary position or as a result of the ambivalence within the party towards the granting of independence to India, were unable to do much of a practical nature to satisfy the demands of Indian nationalists.

There is, as we have noted, another way of looking at all of this. It is possible to see the whole process of reform from the Morley–Minto measures of 1908–9 to the Government of India Act of 1935 as an astute imperial strategy serving to disguise Britain's determination to hang on to India for as long as possible.

Certainly the Montagu–Chelmsford Reforms of 1919 can be seen in that way. On the surface, the concessions appeared substantial: three out of the seven ministers on the Viceroy's Executive Council were now Indian; the 1919 Government of India Act considerably enlarged the Indian electorate, creating Indian majorities in the great provincial councils; in the provincial governments, administrations ruling huge regions like Bengal, the United Provinces, or Madras, a system of dyarchy was introduced whereby Indian and British ministers shared ministerial office.

Closer examination, however, reveals a more complex picture. Although after the implementation of dyarchy,

Indian ministers were given their share of ministries, they were allotted only 'safe' portfolios such as education, public health, agriculture, and irrigation. It was British ministers who held key offices, those necessary to the control of the state, like justice, police, and revenue. In any event, the Viceroy, who was invariably British, could veto legislation passed in the provincial legislatures, suspend provincial councils, and if necessary rule as an autocrat with the backing of the armed services. This residual viceregal prerogative remained in force up to independence in 1947.

Constitutional reforms, at both central and provincial government level, can also be seen as a means of binding India's elites and educated groups to the status quo. It was hoped that Indian ministers and council members would acquire the taste for office and local influence, and seek to preserve rather than to destroy the constitutional structure that delivered these advantages to them. On this analysis, democratic reform became the means by which a fundamentally autocratic British Raj could more comfortably be sustained in power.

The process of constitutional reform also seemed to present the British with a further variation in the old game of 'divide and rule'. The competition for the jobs and responsibilities to which Indians could now aspire, in local as well as central government, potentially increased the chances of communal, provincial, and ethnic rivalry. In many ways, of course, the British had no need to 'divide and rule' in India; the subcontinent was sufficiently divided to begin with. All that was necessary was for the Raj to exploit the gaping and often painful divisions within Indian society as a whole. The devolution of power offered opportunities to utilize such differences, such as in the creation of a separate Muslim electoral roll in the 1909 Indian Councils Act, a move that was arguably ultimately to bear the bitter fruit of Muslim separatism and the partition of the subcontinent in 1947.

The sort of opportunities that the British authorities had for fomenting discord within the nationalist movement is neatly illustrated by the viceroyalty of Lord Reading, between 1921 and 1926. Arriving in India as the Gandhian-led non-cooperation movement was running into difficulties, Reading promptly tried to drive a wedge between India's two main religious groups, the Hindus and the Muslims, who had achieved a surprising level of cooperation in their campaign against the Raj since the groundbreaking Lucknow Pact of 1916.

The Viceroy held a series of informal meetings with Gandhi, hoping to persuade him to renounce the violent political activity associated with some extreme Muslim nationalists. An antipathy to violent political activity was at the root of Gandhi's philosophy. Under pressure from Reading, he agreed to the Viceroy's request that he should obtain a commitment from two leading Muslim activists, the Ali brothers, that they would cease their incitements to violence and apologize publicly for their earlier provocative actions.

Satisfying though this symbolic distancing between Gandhi and Muslim militants was to the Raj, not a great deal came of it in the medium term. In fact, the Ali brothers soon retracted their apology, and Gandhi resumed his offensive against the Raj. Reading had nonetheless at least begun to engineer a 'collapse of the bridge over the gulf between Muslim and Hindu'.

The eagerness of Lord Reading to meet Gandhi was a clear indication of the British authorities' belief that, for all the trouble he was causing, Gandhi, through his consistent opposition to violent action, was a nationalist leader with whom business could be done. Gandhi also gave Reading the clearest explanation as to why Indian nationalism remained suspicious of the Raj's reforms. As Reading recounted to the Prime Minister, David Lloyd George:

> I asked the question point blank: 'What is it in the actions of the Government that makes you pursue the policy of non-cooperation with the Government?' The answer, repeated more than once during our interviews, was that he was filled with distrust of the Government and that all their actions, even though apparently good, made him suspect their motives. I pressed him to be more precise, and eventually he stated that he had some time ago arrived at the conclusion that every action of the Government which appeared good, and indeed was good, was actuated by the

sinister motive of trying to fasten British dominion on India. This was his answer to all the arguments about the new reformed Councils, and in my judgement is the root cause of his present attitude to the Government.[11]

Gandhi was not alone in his jaundiced view of British motives. It was still possible, however, to see the better, more constructive side of the inter-war process of reform. By the mid-1920s, for example, the Raj had committed itself to a policy of Indianization for the Civil Service, the police, and the Indian Army. It was hard to see this as anything but a practical gesture of good intent. It amounted to setting a timetable for India's progress to full independence.

The rate of progress for these reforms was, admittedly, slow: the 1924 Royal Commission on Indianization recommended that the Indian Civil Service should be half-Indian within fifteen years, by 1939, and that the police force should become half-Indian within twenty-five years—that is, by 1949. The Indianization of the army was a far more contentious issue, for obvious security reasons. A number of proposals were rejected by the British government, and opposed by high-ranking British officers within the Indian Army, but an eventual compromise was reached by 1926, when it was agreed that the Indian Army would be half-Indianized by 1952.

Although these proposals failed to satisfy many Indian nationalists, the plans for the Indianization of the

Indian Civil Service undoubtedly had the effect of frightening off British recruits. From 1919 the numbers of British applicants who wished to join the ICS fell away dramatically. This was undoubtedly a significant development. If the recently graduated products of Oxbridge and the British public-school system were clearly indicating from 1919 that they believed India held no long-term career prospects for them, then the writing was indeed upon the wall.

Interestingly, though, this indication that members of Britain's ruling elite so self-evidently believed that the game was up in India must be set against the contra-indication that the British government, British industry, and British investors were conspiring to fight a rearguard and covert action against Indian demands for self-rule.

All this indicates once more how much confusion there was over British aims and practical realities. As a result, the inter-war years were marked by all the contradiction, ambivalence, and tension that had characterized the previous two decades of Indian history. The British, whether in India or at home, reflected many shades of opinion. Although reactionaries were quick to denounce the process of devolution, there were many others who thought differently.

In 1932, for example, the 23-year-old Ian Scott, destined to be an influential key player as Deputy Private Secretary to the Viceroy during the last years of the Raj, left Britain to take up his first posting knowing that 'the Indian political parties wanted us away; but then I agreed with that too'. He also had a sharp dispute on the voyage out with the wife of one of Calcutta's most prosperous businessmen, who refused point blank to have an Indian friend of Scott's sit at the same table on the grounds that her husband 'would divorce her if he found out'. She also asserted that she would 'never let an Indian into her house'. On being asked about servants in Calcutta, she admitted that she employed twenty-three of these—but clearly felt that they did not count as people. Later, however, she consented to a meeting with Scott's Indian friend and found him to be so agreeable that she spent a considerable amount of time in his company.[12]

Such contrary British reactions were still commonplace in the inter-war years. Above all, were Indians really up to taking over, even in the long term? Were they not still intrinsically 'uncivilized', perhaps incapable of being civilized? As a character in the 1935 novel *The Passionate Problem* complains of her servants: 'Half of them don't believe in germs and the other half is too indolent to be enlightened.'[13] Even some Indian observers were unsure on the potential of the lower castes, as in M. J. Anand's 1936 novel *The Coolie*, where the uncouth hill boy Munoo is taken into the service of an aspiring Indian bank clerk, where he soon outrages his employers by defecating outside the house, causing his mistress to wail: 'What will

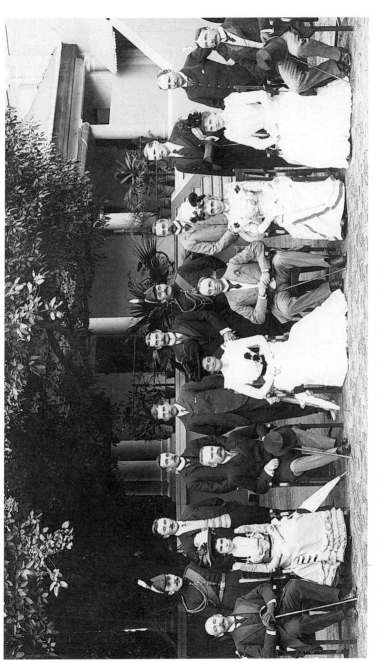

22. 'Superior Person?' Viceroy Lord Curzon (seated fourth from right) held office from 1898–1905

23. Hunters, including the crack-shot King-Emperor George V, 1st left, take a break, 1911

24. Big game hunting in the interwar period. Hunting became a ritual symbolic of British power

25. The Viceroy's House (in fact a vast palace), designed by Edwin Lutyens in 1912

EUROPEAN LADIES

26. European ladies sectioned off during a lavish ceremonial event at the palace of an Indian prince

27. A British family with Guy
Fawkes on 5 November,
in the late 1930s. British
traditions were kept up
faithfully

28. Portrait of Sir Rabindranath
Tagore, Indian poet,
philosopher and Nobel
Prize winner

29. Indian cavalry during the First World War

30. The charismatic nationalist leader, M. K. Gandhi (centre, wearing spectacles) in 1930

31. Passive resistance by Indian nationalists, 1930

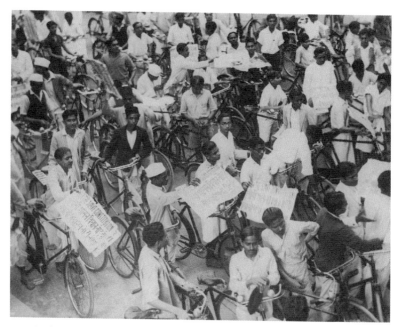

32. Cyclists join a general strike in an act of civil disobedience against British rule, Bombay, 1937

33. Indian tank crews during the Second World War

34. Indian troops lent massive support to Britain during both World Wars

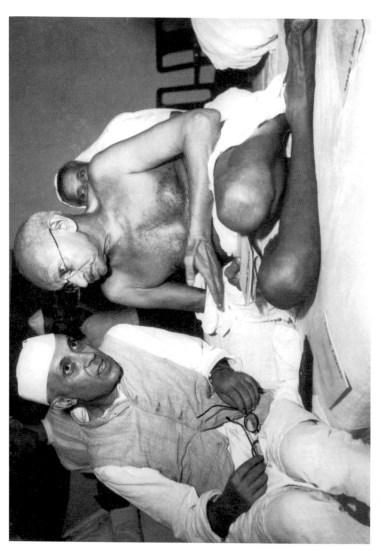

35   Jawaharlal Nehru and Gandhi dicuss tactics, Bombay 1946

36   The savage Hindu-Muslim riots in Calcutta, 1946

37. Lord and Lady Mountbatten; the last Viceroy and Vicereine, 1947

38. Independence day celebrations, Calcutta, August 1947

39. Countless refugees walk to their new homelands after the 1947 partition

40. Partition and its tragic aftermath; Muslim refugees shelter in the Juma Mosque in Delhi, 1947

41. The last British troops dip their flags in a final parade before leaving India in March 1948

the sahibs think who pass by our doors every morning and afternoon? The Babuji has prestige to keep up with the sahibs!'[14]

On the more exalted level of national politics, Indian nationalism was also confused and divided. A majority of the Congress Party opposed what they described as 'council-entry', under the post-1919 constitution. Worse still, a minority broke away to form the *Swaraj* party and sought separate representation in the central and provincial legislatures. For a while a Swarajist majority attempted to obstruct the work of the central legislature, but the Government of India, which was not responsible to that body, carried on regardless.

Amid this uncertainty and disarray, Lord Birkenhead, the Conservative Secretary of State for India during the mid-1920s, ridiculed the idea of a responsible system of government at the centre, stating that it was 'frankly inconceivable that India would ever be fit for Dominion self-government'. Indian nationalist feelings were further inflamed by Birkenhead's decision to appoint a Statutory Commission to investigate the workings of the 1919 reforms. In an act of monumental tactlessness, or perhaps as an indication of Birkenhead's low opinion of Indian capacities, the Commission, under the chairmanship of Sir John Simon, chose not to appoint any Indian members. In response to this slight, a committee under Motilal Nehru, the father of Jawaharlal, produced an alternative report, which demanded immediate self-government within the British Commonwealth.

In 1929 the second Labour minority government came to office. Labour's more conciliatory and generous policy towards India's constitutional aspirations enabled the Viceroy, Lord Irwin (1926–31), a high-minded high Tory, to make an unequivocal gesture of friendship towards India and 'so to restore faith in the ultimate purpose of British policy'.

This conciliatory gesture included a clear statement, the Irwin Declaration, that the natural end of India's constitutional progress, as contemplated in the Montagu Declaration of 1917, was the attainment of Dominion status. Since the 1926 Imperial Conference had thrashed out a definition of Dominion status that effectively gave them complete self-government within the Empire-Commonwealth, this was a glittering prize for Indian nationalists to grasp.

A further significant concession to Indian nationalism took the form of an announcement in October 1929 of a Round Table Conference, at which the princely states and all sections of opinion in British India would be represented, to discuss the means of achieving further constitutional progress. Two more meetings were held in 1930 and 1932.

Although Congress blew hot and cold over the conferences and in protest failed to attend all of them, the upshot was reasonably satisfying from the nationalist point of view. After protracted and sometimes passionate debate in the British Parliament, where Churchill's blood-curdling prophesies of a looming Indian catastrophe led Premier Baldwin to describe him as 'quite mad', there emerged, from the millions of words spoken and written on the subject, the 1935 Government of India Act.

The passing of the 1935 Act seemed virtually to guarantee India independence in the near future. Under the new constitution, although the Raj still kept control of central government, in the eleven provinces power was handed over to elected legislative assemblies and the executive councils that derived from them. This was in effect home rule in the provinces based on the hallowed devolutionary principle of responsible government. In the general elections that followed in 1937, when the 1935 Act came into force, Congress swept the board, winning overall control of seven provinces and power sharing in several others.

The success of Congress was destined to turn sour within a decade. Many of India's Muslims became alarmed at the prospect of the British Raj being replaced by what they feared would turn out to be a Hindu Raj. The Muslim League, which had performed poorly in the 1937 elections, had earlier invited Muhammad Ali Jinnah to return from his comfortable life in Britain and lead them. When after the elections Jinnah tried to set up coalition governments in some provinces with the triumphant

Congress Party, they rejected him, arguing—accurately— that the Muslim League did not represent all Muslims. As a result, Jinnah began a campaign of wooing all Muslim voters—especially those who supported Congress, or other minor Muslim parties. His aim was to make the Muslim League the undisputed party of all of India's Muslims, and himself their 'sole spokesman'.

Before these and other difficulties could be resolved, however, the British Empire was obliged in September 1939 to go to war with Nazi Germany and Fascist Italy.

9

'Engine of War' or the Enemy Within? India, 1939–1945

The outbreak of war in September 1939 violently shattered the relatively cosy impression that India was poised on the brink of Dominion status and independence. Although India had been treated as a proto-Dominion since 1917, and had been granted substantial international recognition at the end of the First World War, including membership of the League of Nations, this was to count for nothing as the war began.

Without consulting a single Indian nationalist leader, the Viceroy, Lord Linlithgow, abruptly announced that war had broken out between the King-Emperor and Germany. Despite the relatively democratic apparatus installed as a result of the 1935 Government of India Act, no consultative or democratic process was followed. India's status was suddenly and shamefully exposed: essentially that of a dependency over whom the Viceroy could rule as an autocrat. Much Indian goodwill, especially within Congress, was lost as a result of this high-handed official attitude to the country's involvement in the war.

The Muslim League, however, increasingly anxious at the success of the Hindu-dominated Congress Party, was more prepared to cooperate with Britain. Congress, whose leading members, particularly Jawaharlal Nehru, were strongly anti-fascist, tried to find a formula by which they could assert India's nationalism and at the same time support the war effort. It was not long, though, before the Congress ministries that ruled in most of the provinces felt obliged to resign in protest over the way in which India had been brought into the war. As a result, the Indian Civil Service, with mixed feelings, once more took up the traditional administrative duties that it had appeared so recently to have passed over to democratic institutions.

It is not difficult to see why Britain had acted so peremptorily. India was still a vitally important military resource, not least in its almost inexhaustible supply of manpower for what threatened to be a long and uncertain struggle. Britain's possession of India and Ceylon, with their fully functional army, air force, and naval bases, also lent weight and authority to the British presence east of

Suez, despite the relatively new and much vaunted base at Singapore.

In spite of Indian nationalists' anger at the way they had been treated at the war's outset, there was no doubt where the loyalties and political sympathies of most of them lay. The future Prime Minister, Jawaharlal Nehru, returning to India six days after the declaration of war, found strong support for Britain. Even Gandhi, though deploring the inevitable violence, spontaneously sided with Britain's cause against the fascist powers of Germany and Italy.

At the outset of hostilities, the Raj tried to appear as majestic and unruffled as in peacetime. The Viceroy's daughter got married amid a display of great luxury and gorgeous ceremonial, which shocked some India hands like Philip Mason, the historian of the Indian Army, who declared the show 'magnificent' but inappropriate for wartime. The Indian civil servant Ian Scott observed: 'The war did not hit India with a bang; the C-in-C. of the Indian Army remained on holiday to finish his week's fishing in Kashmir. In our little corner, the most immediate effect was that prices in the Mansehra bazaar rose at once.'[1] This sangfroid was to last more or less until the unexpected and shocking Japanese attack on Pearl Harbor in December 1941.

Until Japan's assault on Britain's eastern Empire during 1942, the war must have seemed remote and irrelevant for the Indian masses. Price rises and food shortages naturally made an impact, but the wartime aims and principles that galvanized their rulers would have appeared alien and essentially European. Although Gandhi was to say shortly after the beginning of the war, 'We do not seek our independence out of Britain's ruin. That [is] not the way of non-violence,' many others Indians were less high-minded.

Of the hundreds of thousands of fresh recruits into the Indian armed forces, many were motivated by little more than the desire for regular pay and membership of an honourable profession. The general who supervised recruitment into the Indian Army, Sir Robert Lockhart, noted realistically: 'The bulk of the Indian army are . . . pure mercenaries, not activated by love of country or devotion to a distant throne or hatred of the enemy.'[2] Worse still, within a few months of the war's beginning there were several mutinies by Indian troops—in Cairo, Bombay, and Hong Kong. Although the British authorities were quick to blame Communist agitators, this was only a partial explanation of complex and sometimes irrational motives. Sectarian fears also surfaced at this time, as when some Punjabi Sikh troops protested that, if they were moved away on war duties, local Punjabi Muslims would attack their villages and rape their women.

Nehru and other Congress leaders soon decided to equivocate in their attitude to the war, however, in effect asking the Viceroy, in return for cooperation in the war effort, to make a statement that India would be free to determine its own destiny at the end of hostilities. But Lord Willingdon was in no mood to bargain, instead believing that discussion of all constitutional issues should be suspended for the war's duration. Perhaps the Viceroy lost the chance to begin a more creative and mature relationship with Indian nationalism as a result.

Indian nationalism was profoundly agitated by Winston Churchill's succession to the premiership in June 1940. The accession to so powerful a post posed an exquisite dilemma both to the Government of India and to the forces of Indian nationalism. The nationalists' worst fears seemed confirmed when the incoming Prime Minister declared: 'I have not become First Minister of the Crown in order to preside over the liquidation of the British Empire.' He had also described Congress scathingly— and inaccurately—as 'that Hindu priesthood', and had insisted, shortly before becoming Prime Minister, that 'he did not share the anxiety to encourage and promote unity between the Hindu and Muslim communities', adding that 'he regarded the Hindu–Muslim feud as the bulwark of British rule in India'.[3]

Churchill was, however, also a shrewd and pragmatic leader. He knew that he could not fight Hitler and Mussolini with one hand while crushing Indian nationalism with the other. He needed India as an 'engine of war', not as a rebellious hotbed of revolution and dissent. In any event, the Wartime Coalition Government, which he led, included leading Labour and Liberal statesmen, who would not have allowed such a brutal attack upon Indian nationalist sensibilities.

It was soon evident that Churchill was prepared to pay the necessary price to keep India sufficiently loyal, and to put its human and material resources at the disposal of the imperial war effort. During the inter-war years, Churchill had won the reputation of a diehard imperialist determined to obstruct India's progress towards Dominion status at almost any cost. Now the incoming Prime Minister did his best to appear, at least in public, as a leader who, though sometimes disapproving, was understanding of Indian nationalism's difficulties. Not all was as it seemed, however. Churchill's apparent acceptance of the inevitability of India's achievement of independence was largely a device, disguising a deep-rooted inclination to hold on to India for as long as possible. He was soon plotting to undermine and delay the drive towards devolution.

Despite the crisis after the fall of France in the summer of 1940, and the resulting German triumph in Western Europe, despite the Blitz and the desperate struggle to avoid invasion that was ended only by victory during the Battle of Britain, by December 1941 the Empire-Commonwealth had at least held its own. The Italians had been ejected from Abyssinia and Italian Somaliland. German and Italian ambitions in North Africa had been contained, and, as a result, the Suez Canal was still safely in British hands. The *Wehrmacht*'s plunge into the heart of Soviet Russia in July 1941, moreover, had opened up an Eastern Front that was in due course to help bleed Germany dry.

In the Middle East, an anti-British regime in Iraq, determined to rid the country of the Royal Air Force base and of British influence in general, had been ousted by an invasion in 1943. As a consequence, Iraq entered the war on the side of the Allies. In Palestine, although some Arab nationalists attempted to make the most of Nazi Germany's persecution of the Jews, they lacked the strength to oust the British administration. In Persia, an Anglo-Russian partition of the country, very much on the lines of the 'spheres of influence' established in 1907, kept another important Middle Eastern country, and a significant supplier of oil, free from German control.

The Japanese attack on the American naval base at Pearl Harbor in December 1941 made the conflict truly a world war. It also meant that the Allied cause would triumph with the formation of the Grand Alliance between the Soviet Union, the United States, and the British Empire. Allied strength, in material, manpower, and productivity, was now irresistible.

But 1941 also marked the beginning of a series of Japanese victories, which during 1942 wrecked the European empires in South-East Asia and the South Pacific.

The British, French, and Dutch empires in the East collapsed like so many tottering houses of cards—the ignominious surrender of the great fortress of Singapore was particularly humiliating for Britain. Thereafter, as the forces of the imperial powers were scattered like dust, anti-imperial sentiment in the conquered territories was turned to their own short-term advantage by Japan. Japanese military success sowed confusion amongst nationalist movements in Asia: some were prepared to welcome the Japanese as liberators, while others were soon disillusioned by Japanese brutality and by the subordination of the economic and material resources of conquered countries to Japan's war needs.

Japan's triumph was doomed to be short lived. Even the apparently crushing blow dealt at Pearl Harbor was not all it seemed, since American aircraft carriers—which were to provide the chief means of victory in the subsequent naval war in the Pacific—had largely escaped destruction. All the same, victory, was still three and a half years off.

In 1942, with Japanese forces having overrun Burma and crossed the border into Assam, and with bombs falling on Calcutta and other eastern seaboard Indian cities, the Government of India and Indian nationalist leaders struggled to come to an arrangement that would make India more secure. In the middle of 1942, Churchill dispatched a leading Labour member of the War Cabinet, Sir Stafford

Cripps, to India to try to stabilize the position there. US pressure on the British government undoubtedly played a part in the sending of the Cripps Mission.

Earlier in 1942, President Roosevelt, meeting Churchill aboard the Royal Navy battleship *Prince of Wales*, off the coast of Newfoundland, had obliged the British Prime Minister to sign the Atlantic Charter. This agreement was in some respects an updated version of President Woodrow Wilson's attempt in 1918 to shift the imperial agenda from the traditional mechanics of colonial control to that of trusteeship, and to achieve a consistent devolution of imperial power under international supervision. The Atlantic Charter did not go quite that far, but it undoubtedly signified the determination of the USA to act as the midwife and guarantor of colonial liberties and to drag a supplicant Britain along in the process. Roosevelt held the British Empire in low esteem, and claimed that 'the British would take land anywhere in the world, even if it were only a rock or a sandbar'.

It was, therefore, not surprising that the Atlantic Charter included a reference to 'the right of all people to choose the form of Government under which they live'. Although Churchill tried to exempt the British Empire from this stout declaration of principle, he failed, and on his return to Britain was reduced to the blustering and misleading assertion that it 'was primarily intended to apply to Europe'. The Cripps Mission, however, was plainly a by-product of the Atlantic Charter, and an attempt to buy American approval.

The Cripps Mission partly placated American anti-imperial feeling, particularly within the Democratic government. It also destabilized Indian politics. There is no doubt that Churchill chose to see the Mission as doomed from the outset, and furthermore did his best to sabotage it. Cripps offered India's nationalists post-war independence—either within the Commonwealth or outside it—the right of Muslim-majority provinces to opt out of an independent India, and the immediate inclusion of Indian leaders in the Government of India. After some agonizing, Congress decided to reject the plan, and a disappointed and humiliated Cripps returned to the United Kingdom.

Chiefly as a result of the failure of the Cripps Mission, and inspired by Gandhi—who insisted that the British must now leave India so that a purified subcontinent could the better resist the Japanese through the power of *satyagraha*—Congress passed its 'Quit India' resolution in August 1942, and also called for the immediate dismantling of the Raj. In reprisal, the British authorities arrested hundreds of Congress leaders, thus cutting off the party's head. Violent protest occurred throughout India, causing the Viceroy, Lord Linlithgow, to describe the disturbances as 'the worst since the Mutiny'. The Raj, aided by the still loyal Indian Army and the Indian police, eventually restored order. The Indian Empire continued to make a significant contribution to the winning of the war.

The arrest and imprisonment of so many leaders of the Congress Party, however, created a vacuum in the Indian political scene. Into the vacuum stepped the Muslim League, led by the anglicized, ascetic Muhammad Ali Jinnah. Jinnah, who had partly quit Congress fearing that Gandhi's domination of the movement would deny him supreme political power, followed up Congress's 'Quit India' resolution with one from the Muslim League demanding that Britain 'Divide and Quit'.

Ignoring the League's resolution, the British proceeded to play the Muslim card. The new Viceroy, Field Marshal Sir Archibald Wavell, vigorously promoted cooperation between India's Muslims and the Raj. A disproportionate 30 per cent of the Indian Army was Muslim, and the Punjab, with its population divided between Sikhs and Muslims, was one of the Raj's main recruiting grounds. When the Muslim League wanted to found a party newspaper, *Dawn*, the Government of India proceeded to subsidize it through the placing of substantial amounts of advertisements within its pages.

From the 'Quit India' resolution of August 1942 until the end of the war, the Muslim League campaigned hard to woo the majority of Muslim voters away from Congress and over to them. Their tactics were simple: they painted a grim picture of an independent India dominated by the Hindu majority within Congress. Their remedy was equally straightforward: the creation of the safe haven of a Muslim homeland—Pakistan. Their success was to be crucial in the slow and confused process that was eventually to lead to the partition of India and the creation of the independent state of Pakistan. The British need for wartime allies fed directly into this, thus ironically undermining their desire to leave their Indian Empire as a unified, secular state.

An even more threatening and disruptive development for the Raj was the formation of the Indian National Army (INA) in 1942. This was the brainchild of the disaffected and brilliant rising Congress star Subhas Chandra Bose. From a prosperous Bengali background, and the recipient of a first-rate British education, Bose, inspired by his ambitious father, was early on marked out as a man of destiny in the struggle for Indian independence. The path to the top, however, was not an open road. Eventually in 1942, despairing of leading Congress to independence while the equally brilliant Jawaharlal Nehru was the obvious favourite of Gandhi and the party majority, Bose took the extraordinary step of approaching the governments of Japan and Germany to ask for support in waging a war against the British.

The deal Bose offered the fascist Axis powers, in return for their support, was a full-scale military uprising aimed at toppling the Raj and igniting Indian dissent. He recruited about 50,000 Indian prisoners-of-war from Japanese prison camps—not too hard a task given the appalling conditions that prevailed in most of them. Armed and equipped by Japan, the INA was for a time a thorn in Britain's side in India, and offered a dramatic, non-Gandhian way of opposing the Raj.

In the end, the challenge melted away with the increasing tide of Allied military success in Asia. Bose's cause was not helped by his flying to Berlin for a personal meeting with Hitler. Far from offering copious aid, the Führer was dismissive of Bose's ambitions and briskly informed him that what India needed was 'another hundred years of British rule' in order to 'civilize' it![4]

By the war's end, the Raj's main preoccupation was how far to seek judicial redress against those INA volunteers who had surrendered. Legally treason had been committed. Anxious not to inflame Indian nationalism further, the British eventually decided to arrange a symbolic trial of a Hindu, a Muslim, and a Sikh drawn from the INA, and to pardon all other offenders. The affair was to be finally tidied up by the official destruction of a memorial to the INA erected in Singapore.

As the war went badly for the Japanese in the Far East and South-East Asia, and as the battles of El Alamein and Stalingrad in the West proved to be turning points in the Allied campaigns there, the forces of the Axis powers were driven back. The British reconquest of Burma, Malaya, Borneo, and Hong Kong met little resistance, even from those local groups that had collaborated with the Japanese. Clearly Britain's Empire in Asia would be restored in full.

As final victory approached, however, Britain's imperial standing was complicated by the fact that both the United States and the Soviet Union were carrying an increasing and ultimately dominant share of the war effort, and that neither of these great powers had any affection for British imperialism. The Russians, of course, despite their own expanding, imperial frontiers, were antipathetic towards the British Empire from conviction based upon Marxist ideology. The United States had a lengthy history of disliking and mistrusting Imperial Britain, even though the Americans had possessed their own empire in the Caribbean and the Pacific since the late nineteenth century. Churchill, in his role as one of the 'Big Three' Allied war leaders, frequently found himself squeezed by pressure from both the Soviet Union and the United States. As he ruefully observed: 'There is only one thing worse than fighting with allies, and that is fighting without them.'

Not that the Government of India's support for the war effort had been unconditional. When war broke out in September 1939, the British government even agreed to pay for the out-of-ordinary costs of using the Indian Army, a concession that resulted eventually in a £1.3 billion British debt to India, amounting to approximately one-fifth of Britain's gross national product. It was hard to see how Britain, now a debtor to its great Indian possession, could still behave as if it ruled the roost.

Nonetheless, the Raj carried on more or less as before. Despite the pressures and privations of total war, it appeared to be as stately and almost as assured as ever. Even before the defeat of Japan, however, Britain had held a general election in the summer of 1945. To the surprise of many, Churchill was pitched out of office as the result of a landslide for Labour. Indian nationalists greeted the new government with relief and optimism since many Labour leaders had a history of strong support for the process of Indian self-determination. The surprising thing was, however, that the achievement of independence turned out to be over two years away.

10

'Tryst with Destiny': Freedom and Partition, 1945–1947

Indian nationalists were at first disappointed with the incoming Labour government in Britain. Although 'Labour entered office keen to fulfil the promise of early self-government for India . . . their imperialist inheritance was an impediment.' Far from dismantling the Empire, the Attlee administration took some time to marshal its thoughts on the Indian problem and to move towards a satisfactory resolution. This led to yet more delay in the achievement of independence.

Despite much pre-election anti-imperialistic rhetoric, and the genuine encouragement of colonial freedom movements by Labour politicians and activists during the inter-war years, once in power the Attlee Cabinet was determined to behave responsibly on the issue of Empire.

In this regard, despite the government's huge overall majority, it was little different from Ramsay MacDonald's two previous minority Labour administrations.

One obvious reason for this cautious approach in 1945 to the encouragement and implementation of colonial freedom lay in the conservative views of a number of leading ministers; chief among these were Ernest Bevin and Herbert Morrison. Nor was the Prime Minister, taciturn, inscrutable, and pipe smoking, a revolutionary bent on the prompt dissolution of the British Empire.

Nationalist leaders such as Nehru had earlier made personal contact with leading members of the Labour Party, like Sir Stafford Cripps, during his visit to Britain in June 1938. In Britain, Nehru had met Clement Attlee, Aneurin Bevan, and members of Labour's Shadow Cabinet, as well as the influential Harold Laski, a Professor at the London School of Economics and a member of the National Executive Committee. Despite these contacts, once in office, even the passionately left-wing Bevan had prevaricated over Indian independence, causing the Viceroy, Field Marshal Lord Wavell, caustically to observe in December 1946: 'Bevan like everyone else hates the idea of our leaving India, but like everyone else has no alternative to suggest.'[1]

Many of the British in India felt the same, though there were complaints of the 'country going to the dogs' as the Raj's power waned. British women in particular found their servants more insolent and often expressed fears of attack and rape. Simultaneously, many Indian civil servants and politicians were staking out their claims for favourable treatment and advancement once the British had gone. Things seemed rapidly to be falling apart. As a Congress politician remarked to the Viceroy Lord Wavell, 'Nobody worships the setting sun.'

The army in particular did not relish its last few years of peace keeping, especially as violence occurred and Indians became more dissident and 'uppity' than before. A Sergeant A. B. Davies wrote to his Labour MP at home: 'Many of us sympathise with the Indian cause. We Socialists in the Army, and there are many, are in a difficult position. Let not the people at home, therefore, blame us if they find that "authority" finds that it has to deal with us, as well with the Indian people.'[2] A Private Blackie, on the other hand, told his parents on Tyneside: 'If there is one thing that makes an Indian's legs turn to water it is the sight of a bayonet.' But other British troops told a visiting MP that 'If this is what India is like and the Indians do not want us, what are we here for and why do we bother to fight?'[3]

When eventually these troops were being shipped home, Indian and British leaders may have been finding graceful and even warm things to say about each other, but the feelings of the rank and file were somewhat different. 'Cheer, wogs! We are quitting India', was a slogan chalked on carriages carrying troops to their embarkation points. As the 1st Cameron Highlanders marched away they sang:

> Land of shit and filth and wogs
> Gonorrhea, syphilis, clap and pox.
> Memsahibs'paradise, soldiers' hell
> India fare thee fucking well.[4]

Before the British could depart, however, a solution had to be found to the political stalemate in India. Inevitably, the Labour administration of 1945–51 was primarily concerned with its radical programme of nationalization and the creation of the Welfare State. The mass of the voters who had put Labour into power did not necessarily know, when they considered it at all, whether they wanted an indefinite extension of the Raj and the British Empire. What they plainly did want was the rapid demobilization of the armed forces, together with full employment and the reassuring establishment of the Welfare State.

For the last few months of 1945, the Labour government in effect marked time, prudently waiting to see the outcome of the central and provincial Indian elections fixed for the end of the year. The last elections for the central assembly had been held as long ago as 1934 and for the provincial legislatures in 1937. The new elections would provide, among other things, a crucial indication of the electoral strength of the Muslim League. During the campaign, Jinnah and his supporters went all out for a result that would establish beyond all reasonable doubt the necessity of creating a Muslim homeland, to be called Pakistan. In the process, the Muslim nightmare of a united India dominated by an unsympathetic Hindu majority was vividly and unscrupulously conjured up—'the Hindu Raj', as Muslim propagandists described it.

For its part, Congress made its usual broad appeal to a wide spectrum of interests. A surprisingly low-key election campaign was given an unexpected shot in the arm by the Government of India's apparent determination to put on trial and suitably punish those who had taken up arms in Bose's Indian National Army. Although most nationalist leaders had, at best, ambivalent attitudes towards the INA, they saw in the Government's public vindictiveness a chance to raise the issue to their electoral advantage. As early as August 1945, Nehru had argued that the soldiers of the INA should not be treated as ordinary rebels, and that to punish them 'would in effect be a punishment on all India and all Indians, and a deep wound would be created in millions of hearts'.

By the middle of September 1945 the All India Congress Committee came out in defence of the accused officers, arguing that they were guilty only of 'having laboured, however mistakenly, for the freedom of India'. A Defence Committee was set up by Congress to help those accused. The British authorities pushed ahead, however, with a show trial, which was staged in November 1945 in the Red Fort at Delhi. Three former Indian Army officers who had held high rank in the INA were charged with, in effect, treason. With either exquisite sensibility or extreme tactlessness, of the three officers accused one was a Hindu, one a Muslim, and the third a Sikh. India's three major religious communities were thus all likely to be equally antagonized by the trial.

Despite a spirited and complex defence, the accused men were found guilty and sentenced to be cashiered and transported for life to penal settlements. There was an immediate outcry and the British authorities backed down, remitting the sentences of transportation, although confirming the other penalties. It was also announced that there would be no more trials of returning INA soldiers, except those accused of atrocities.

Congress, through its resolute defence of the accused, had won a significant propaganda victory and had revitalized its electoral appeal. Unfortunately for those who still hoped for a free and united India, Congress's renewed appeal to the electorate only succeeded in pushing Jinnah and the League into making the issue of partition and the establishment of Pakistan central to the election. Muslim separatism was further provoked by the impression given by some Congress leaders that, once the British had gone, they would resolve the communal conflict themselves, by 'civil war if necessary'.

The result of the 1945–6 elections confirmed the remarkable progress of the Muslim League. In the central assembly the League won all the reserved Muslim seats, with 86.6 per cent of the vote. In the provinces where Muslims formed the majority of the population, however, the League did not win a majority of votes. Its vote in the Punjab, for instance, was 46.56 per cent and in Sind 45.75 per cent, while in the North West Frontier Province it succeeded in achieving only 37.19 per cent. But in terms of seats gained, the League did spectacularly, perhaps unfairly well. Nonetheless Congress was able to form ministries in eight of the eleven provinces, and the League only in Bengal and Sind, with the Punjab ruled by a coalition Unionist Party supported by Congress. As a result, however, Jinnah's claim that the Muslim League was the true, indeed the only, voice of Islam in India seemed to have sufficiently firm foundations. With conflict looming between Congress and the League, the Labour government's somewhat indecisive response was to send a parliamentary delegation to reassure Indians of the Cabinet's sincerity of purpose.

Before this could happen, the government was violently shaken out of its apparent lethargy by the mutinies of early 1946. The first of these, in the middle of January, was all the more shocking as it took place among British RAF servicemen infuriated by delays over demobilization and repatriation. Units of the Indian Air Force were the next to mutiny. Much worse was to follow. In February a naval mutiny broke out at Bombay. The Bombay mutiny was followed by others at Calcutta, at Madras, and at Karachi, where the local army commander actually opened fire on rebel ships, causing considerable casualties.

The mutinies were quite soon quelled, but they had the effect of pushing the Government into action. Attlee announced that a delegation of senior Cabinet ministers would leave directly for India to meet political leaders and to search for a solution to the problems of India's constitutional future. The Cabinet Mission consisted of the Secretary of State for India, Lord Pethick Lawrence (soon derided by his critics as 'Pathetic Lawrence'), Sir Stafford Cripps, and A. V. Alexander, First Lord of the Admiralty. Of these, Cripps, with all his Indian experience, was clearly the key figure.

The job of the Cabinet Mission was to arrange India's orderly progress to independence. The mission would set up appropriate consultative machinery to decide upon the form of the independence constitution. It was entirely up to Indians to decide upon their future form of government. In due course, a Constituent Assembly, composed of delegates elected by the provincial assemblies, would draft an all-India constitution.

Significantly, if any province chose to opt out of the proceedings, it would simply be bypassed until it wished to re-enter the negotiations. Whether the state of Pakistan should be established or not would be settled, either by the agreement of the leading political parties, or through a plebiscite of all the inhabitants of the areas concerned. An independent India would also be free to leave the Commonwealth if it so wished.

Soon after arriving in India, the Cabinet Mission realized that the apparently liberal policy of leaving things to Indians to settle for themselves would only end in deadlock and chaos—particularly the disagreement over whether or not a Muslim state should be established.

With neither Congress nor the League able to agree on this crucial issue, the Cabinet Mission put forward its own proposals. These consisted of the establishment of a union government that would deal with foreign affairs, defence, and communications; two groups of provinces, one predominantly Hindu and the other predominantly Muslim, dealing with matters of common interest; and all residuary powers invested in the provinces.

A conference met at Simla to consider whether these proposals formed the basis of a settlement. At the conference, it first appeared that Jinnah was not pressing for the establishment of a separate sovereign state. For his part, Nehru stated that Congress would not compel any Muslim-dominated province to stay in an all-India federation. As a result of this apparent accord, on 8 May 1946 the Cabinet Mission drew up 'Suggested Points for Agreement'. While proposing an all-India government and legislature, composed of equal proportions from the Muslim-majority and Hindu-majority provinces, and dealing with matters such as foreign affairs, defence, and communications, the suggestions included the phrase 'Groups of provinces may be formed'. All parties, including the Viceroy, recognized the phrase 'may be formed' as a vital concession to Congress, since the word 'may' seemed to keep open the door for a united India.

Soon Jinnah was asserting that the question of partition had already been settled by the Muslim vote at the recent elections, but conceded that he was prepared for the sovereignty of Pakistan to be delegated within a loose and limited union, provided that sovereignty was recognized in the form of a group of provinces. Nehru responded that a strong central government was required, and that essentially Congress did not agree with the League on the issue of partition.

Despairing of further progress, the Cabinet Mission re-asserted its own plan. These proposals clearly rejected the idea of partition. There would be an Indian union, dealing with foreign affairs, defence, and communications, with the necessary authority to raise appropriate finance. Any major communal issue brought to the central legislature would require a majority of each community as well as an overall majority before it became law. All other powers would be vested in the provinces, which would be enabled to form groups with a great deal of autonomy. The arrangement of the union and the groupings could be reconsidered every ten years.

There were also clear plans for the election of the Constituent Assembly that would determine the final constitutional settlement. The Cabinet Mission also advocated the immediate formation of an interim government. What the Mission was offering was a mechanism for ending deadlock and enabling India to obtain independence 'in the shortest time and with the least danger of internal disturbance and conflict'. Both Congress and the League proceeded to interpret the plan, particularly the reference to groups, to their own advantage.

Congress was disappointed at the failure to arrive at a speedy and mutually acceptable solution. In addition, there was the problem of the princely states. How were these provinces, some huge and some minute, to be peacefully incorporated into the proposed union of India? Would their frequently autocratic rulers, for so long sustained by the British, willingly set aside their power and allow democracy to flourish? Interestingly, in June 1946, Nehru was actually arrested for illegally crossing the frontier of Kashmir, where the Maharajah had arrested Sheikh Abdullah and other leaders of the National Conference who were either members or supporters of Congress. Although he was soon released, the incident was a demonstration of the continuing power and prejudices of the Indian princes.

At the end of June 1946 the Cabinet Mission departed, leaving Lord Wavell to negotiate the formation of the interim government that was so central a part of the

Mission's plan. It was possible to proceed only on the assumption that both Congress and the League had agreed to the process. Nehru, however, created confusion by asserting the Congress line, 'We are not bound by a single thing except that we have decided to go into the Constituent Assembly.' Jinnah now swooped on Nehru's remarks and used them as a justification for withdrawing the League's apparent acceptance of the plan. The situation was getting ever more complex and confused.

As President of the Congress, Nehru was now asked by the Viceroy to submit proposals for the formation of an interim government and, if possible, to get Jinnah to agree to the plans before they were laid on the table. Almost inevitably the Nehru–Jinnah talks failed. For a while it seemed that the British authorities would work with Congress to the detriment of the League, but Wavell would have none of this and sought once more to appease the Muslims. Doubtless he felt justified in making this move by the terrible consequences of the Muslim League's Direct Action Day, called for 16 August 1946. The main trouble spot was Calcutta, where the Muslim League Prime Minister of Bengal, Hussein Shaheed Suhrawardy, displayed a shamefully partisan attitude as the communal killings escalated out of control. By 21 August unofficial estimates put the number of dead, both Hindu and Muslim, at over 15,000. Corpses lay rotting in the streets. Communal rioting spread to other areas.

Against this grim background, Nehru and the Congress leadership firmly insisted that the proposed ministry should be a strong and stable government, even if the League was unwilling to join it. The ministry Nehru wanted consisted of fifteen members, five 'caste Hindus', five Muslims, one scheduled caste, and four minority representatives. He got his way, and the Viceroy announced the list of ministers. Nehru was vice-president of the executive council of this interim government, holding the portfolios of external affairs and Commonwealth relations.

The interim government would lack substance if still boycotted by the League. Urgent attempts were made to bring the Muslim League into the interim administration. Jinnah, who had no desire to be left out of office, was eventually persuaded, after negotiations with Nehru and the granting of some concessions by Congress, that he should join the government. As it happened, the Congress–League accord was disrupted by Wavell, who brought Jinnah and his nominees unconditionally into the government. Although Congress grudgingly accepted this, the interim government was a miserable failure. Congress and the League acted as rival factions, and in any case the executive had little real power.

At the same time it was proving almost impossible to set up the constitution-making Constituent Assembly with the agreement of all parties. After more concessions to the League, however, the body met on 9 December 1946.

Its work was piecemeal and frequently disrupted, particularly by the League. In effect, Jinnah could, by threatening to withdraw, destroy the whole process.

By the end of January 1947 obstruction by the League and by the Indian princes had effectively destroyed the Assembly's work. As communal rioting spread across northern India, the nine non-Muslim League members of the government informed the Viceroy that in their opinion the League could not continue in the administration. Nehru and his colleagues threatened resignation. The Viceroy put pressure on Congress for further concessions. It now seemed that Jinnah, acting as the Muslim's 'sole spokesman', was single-handedly dictating the course of events.

At last the British government acted decisively to resolve the complex crisis. On 20 February 1947 the Prime Minister announced in the House of Commons that the British would withdraw from India no later than June 1948. This meant that there had to be a transfer of power into responsible Indian hands by that date. In February 1947 it was not at all clear whose those hands might be. Addressing this problem, Attlee's statement contained, in effect, an ultimatum: 'His Majesty's Government will have to consider to whom the powers of the Central Government of British India should be handed over, on the due date, whether to some form of Central Government for British India or in some areas to the existing Provincial

Governments, or in such a way as may be most reasonable and in the best interests of the Indian people.'5

In another bold move, the Prime Minister, recognizing Wavell's reputation for pro-Muslim partiality, and growing impatient with his despairing attitude, announced that there would be a new Viceroy. The replacement would be Earl Mountbatten of Burma. This appointment signalled in the most dramatic way the government's determination to break out from the constitutional and communal wranglings of the past and to make a fresh start in India.

Lord Mountbatten was sworn in as Viceroy on 24 March 1947. He had, as it turned out, less than five months to accomplish a transfer of power of a complexity and significance hitherto unknown in British imperial history. This, the last and briefest viceroyalty, was also to be one of the most decisive and momentous. Mountbatten came to his task with unique qualifications. Royal blood flowed in his veins, and it was entirely appropriate that the last Viceroy should also be a great-grandson of Queen Victoria and a cousin of the last King-Emperor George VI.

After a distinguished record of active service in the Royal Navy, Mountbatten had finally been appointed Supreme Allied Commander in South-East Asia. As a consequence, he had an intimate knowledge of Indian forces, the subcontinent, and the surrounding area. It is significant that, when created an Earl, he took the title of

Mountbatten of Burma. As if these qualifications were insufficient, Mountbatten and his intelligent and vivacious wife, Edwina, were known to be Labour sympathizers and in general supporters of the cause of colonial freedom.

Nehru, marked out as the most likely first Prime Minister of an independent India, already knew Mountbatten relatively well. The two men had much in common. They had been born to privilege and power, were used to exercising authority, and were both inclined to shows of personal vanity. There is also some evidence that Nehru saw in Mountbatten another authoritative personality to whom he could become attached, rather as he had with Gandhi—not exactly a father-figure, but certainly one representing power and prestige. At any rate, there could be no doubting the close personal and working relationship that soon developed between the two men.

It also seems clear that a passionate friendship developed between Nehru and Lady Mountbatten. The Mountbattens' marriage had been marked previously by various acts of infidelity on both sides, perhaps more on her part than his. Although historians have haggled over the details, the intimate relationship that developed between Nehru and Lady Mountbatten seems not to have disrupted Jawaharlal's friendship with the Viceroy and, arguably, to have enhanced it. Lord Mountbatten's official biographer writes of a relationship that was 'intensely loving, romantic, trusting, generous, idealistic, even spiritual', although he adds, rather curiously, 'If there was any physical element it can only have been of minor importance to either party.' Mountbatten was later to write to his wife: 'I am very glad that you realise that I know and have always understood the very special relationship between Jawaharlal and you, made easier by my fondness and admiration for him, and by the remarkably lucky fact that among my many defects God did not add jealousy in any shape or form.'[6]

Before long, the Viceroy and his advisers produced a 'Plan Balkan'. In essence, this plan initially devolved power to the provinces, including the princely states, which would then be left to decide whether they would form into any groups, allowing them to negotiate deals with central government before being integrated into what was effectively a weak union. The chaos that could have ensued if such a plan had been implemented can only be imagined. With power at the centre so uncertain, conceivably any number of new states could emerge from the confusion. Quite apart from Pakistan, which the now dying Jinnah and the League were bent on creating at almost any cost, there could have been an independent Hyderabad or Kashmir, and it has been argued that there 'could have been an independent Bengal, and there certainly would have been two Punjabs'. Such a 'Balkanization' would have been a sad, inept, and paradoxical conclusion to nearly two centuries of British centralizing rule.

Mountbatten had originally intended to unveil these proposals at a meeting with Indian Nationalist leaders on 17 May. On 8 May the Viceroy invited Nehru, his daughter, Indira (also destined to be a Prime Minister of India), and Krishna Menon to join him and Lady Mountbatten as personal guests at the Viceregal Lodge at Simla. On the evening of 10 May, Mountbatten, alone in his study with Nehru after dinner, decided, on a 'hunch', as he later described it, to show his guest a copy of the secret plan. It was an act of some recklessness and no doubt derived from the Viceroy's partiality for Congress as opposed to the League. The Viceroy explained his motives frankly, if naively, the next day: 'Last night, having made real friends with Nehru during his stay here, I asked him whether he would look at the London draft, as an act of friendship and on the understanding that he would not utilise his prior knowledge or mention to his colleagues that he had seen it.'

The file's contents horrified Nehru and reduced him to rage and disappointment. The next day he wrote in a 'Personal and Secret' letter to Mountbatten that the proposals had 'produced a devastating effect upon me. . . . The whole approach was completely different from what ours had been and the picture of India that emerged frightened me . . . a picture of fragmentation and conflict and disorder, and, unhappily also, of a worsening of relations between India and Britain.'[7] Understandably dismayed at Nehru's furious reaction, although probably relieved that

he had at least shown him the plan prior to the meeting of
17 May, Mountbatten hastened to mend broken fences.
The 17 May meeting was postponed and he instructed his
advisers to refashion the proposals in a way that would
meet Nehru's and Congress's objections.

The plan that subsequently emerged was acceptable
to Congress because it reasserted the concept of an Indian
state as a continuing entity, while allowing for the seces-
sion of those provinces where the majority of the inhabitants desired such a move. Nor would the plan apply to the
princely states. The Constituent Assembly would continue
to meet, and there would also be a second Constituent
Assembly for those areas that chose not to join in the work
of the existing assembly.

Arrangements were provided for the apparently inevitable partitioning, and the subsequent boundary demarca-
tions of states like Bengal and the Punjab. The continuing
problem of the North West Frontier Province was to be
solved by making a concession to the League. If, as
expected, the Punjab decided on partition, a referendum
would be held in the North West Frontier Province under
the authority of the Governor General and in collaboration with the provincial government.

Jinnah and the Muslim League soon knew about
the apparent collusion between Mountbatten and Nehru.
Secrets were hard to keep in India at the best of times,
but, as British power faded, Indian officials now leaked

information almost as a matter of course. As a result, incensed and disappointed, the League now refused to allow the last Viceroy to become the first Governor General of an independent Pakistan as he was to become of the new India. It is very likely that, if the original plan had been carried out, Mountbatten, with some control over the military forces in Pakistan, could have acted to prevent some of the post-partition communal massacres.

While nationalist leaders were digesting and generally approving the overall constitutional proposals, the horrifying spread of communal violence in places like Lahore and Calcutta caused Nehru and his colleagues to demand an immediate transfer of power in order to bring about a restoration of order. While indicating his sympathy with Nehru's impatience, Mountbatten induced him to agree to the proposed referendum in the North West Frontier Province and also to accept Dominion status rather than republican status. From the outset, the British government and the Viceroy had wanted an independent India, whether partitioned or not, to remain within the Commonwealth. Now, despite some protests from within Congress, the principle of Dominion status was accepted as a means of speeding the transfer of power.

By early June 1947 the British and all the major parties concerned had agreed upon the process to be followed. On the evening of 3 June, Mountbatten broadcast to the nation, outlining the agreement. He was followed by

Nehru, Jinnah, and Baldev Singh, the representative of the Sikhs. Nehru said: 'We are little men serving a great cause, but because the cause is great something of that greatness falls upon us also. Mighty forces are at work in the world today and in India, and I have no doubt that we are ushering in a period of greatness for India. The India of geography, of history and tradition, the India of our minds and hearts, cannot change.'[8]

The date for the transfer of power had been set at 15 August 1947. With the establishment of an independent Pakistan now inevitable, a Partition Committee was set up, chaired by the Viceroy and with a number of representative Indian members. Beneath this committee was a structure of subcommittees and expert committees that would deal with a whole range of topics from the fixing of boundaries to the division of the armed forces.

One particularly tricky problem, however, was the future of the princely states. As British resident agents and their political departments were withdrawn from these provinces, some of them openly prepared for independence, expanding their armies and acquiring modern weapons. Despite the pretensions of some of their rulers, before 15 August, all the princely states except three had acceded to one or other of the two new Dominions. These three were Kashmir, Hyderabad, and Junagadh. Nehru's interest in Kashmir was of an intimate and long-standing nature. Hyderabad was a very large state at the centre of the country, which had even in the recent past sought territorial access to the sea in order to advance its economic future. In contrast, Junagadh was a comparatively small state of some 4,000 square miles on the coast north of Bombay. The problem of these three non-acceding provinces, however, would have to wait for a solution until after the transfer of power.

At midnight on 14 August the British Raj came to an end. As two new nations were born, amid both hope and violence, Nehru made one of his most moving speeches:

> Long years ago we made a tryst with destiny, and now the time comes when we shall redeem our pledge, not wholly or in full measure, but very substantially. At the stroke of the midnight hour, when the world sleeps, India will awake to life and freedom. A moment comes, which comes but rarely in history, when we step out from the old to the new, when an age ends, and when the soul of a nation long suppressed finds utterance.[9]

The pomp and ceremony that attended the transfer of power, and the unaffected joy with which it was greeted, merely masked an unfolding tragedy of enormous dimensions. As millions of people migrated to one or other of the two new Dominions, the communal violence and killings that had been a prelude to independence grew in ferocity and scale.

Nowhere was the bloodshed more horrifying than in the Punjab. Here two of the Raj's most cherished 'martial races' were almost equally divided in two halves of a province rich in historical and religious associations and of great significance in the provision of water for India's thirsty irrigation systems. With the Muslim majority in north Punjab acceding to Pakistan, and the southern Sikh-dominated region cleaving to India, confrontation was probably inevitable. The already tense situation became a crisis as each demonized the other and as tales of mass slaughter, rape, and atrocity burgeoned.

Trainloads of waylaid and murdered refugees steamed into their final destinations, the flies swarming over the corpses and the stench of death hanging over the carriages like a miasma. Wynford Vaughan-Thomas, reporting for the BBC, recalled a senior Indian railway official wringing his hands and bemoaning, not so much the atrocities, but the fact that the famously punctual timetables of the system were now in ruins. The divided province of Bengal suffered equally cruel though less widespread killings. There are varying computations as to how many Indians lost their lives during these terrible mass migrations, but a figure of close to a million seems a reasonable estimate.

Both Nehru and Gandhi did their utmost to put an end to the violence and to protect the rights of minorities. Nehru was the new Prime Minister of independent India, so his voice carried great weight, but the crisis made him once more draw closer to Gandhi as the man who had founded his political career upon the principle of non-violence. The assistance of Mountbatten, as Governor General, was also requested by Nehru, though alas this was not possible in Pakistan.

During the last months of 1947, Nehru paid almost daily visits to Gandhi. The Mahatma himself was greatly agitated by the hideous spectacle of communal violence, and concerned by rumours that Congress politicians were already taking bribes from businessmen and others, profiting from the black market and the like. As a result, Gandhi resorted once more to the weapon of fasting.

At partition and its violent aftermath, Gandhi's peacemaking activities redoubled, as he travelled the land urging Hindus and Muslims to live peacefully with each other. These efforts antagonized many fanatical and fundamentalist Hindus and led to several plots to assassinate him. An attempt to blow him up with a bomb at a prayer meeting on 20 January 1948 failed. During the subsequent interrogations, the police learnt of a continuing plot to assassinate the Mahatma, but inexplicably, and perhaps suspiciously, did very little to follow up their clues.

On 30 January 1948 Gandhi was shot at pointblank range by a young man dressed in khaki who had attracted his attention by calling out 'Bapuji, Bapuji' (Father, Father). The Mahatma gasped, 'Oh, God', and collapsed, to die almost immediately. Mountbatten, when informed of the tragedy amid calls for revenge upon the suspected Muslim assassin, cried out with great presence of mind,

'You fool! Don't you know it was a Hindu?' Although Mountbatten did not know at that moment that the assassin was indeed a Hindu, his quick reaction had the effect of avoiding what could have been another terrible chapter of communal violence and massacre.

Nehru was grief stricken. He rushed to the scene of the assassination, where he 'bent his head down and began to sob like a child'. A few hours later, urged by Mountbatten to broadcast to the nation, Nehru gave a deeply moving and appropriate expression to his grief and to the loss that the death of Gandhi implied:

> Friends and comrades, the light has gone out of our lives and there is darkness everywhere. . . . The light has gone out, I said, and yet I was wrong. For the light that shone in this country was no ordinary light. . . . That light represented something more that the immediate present, it represented the living, the eternal truths, reminding us of the right path, drawing us from error, taking this ancient country to freedom . . . A great disaster is a symbol to us to remember all the good things of life and forget the small things of which we have thought too much. In his death he has reminded us of the big things of life, the living truth, and if we remember that, then it will be well with India.[10]

Thus amid a welter of bloodshed, constitutional haggling, mass migrations, and a frenzy of hope and pain, British rule in India came finally to an end. It was the greatest transfer of power in human history, and it was complete.

Epilogue

Whe British rule finally came to an end, what had it all amounted to? In many ways, the jury is still out. There are sharply different ways of seeing the experience, especially from the viewpoints of rulers and ruled. During the last fifty years, the debate has got under way in earnest, and it is still unfinished business.

There are big and complex questions to confront, like the fundamental query, did Britain develop India or exploit it? In whose interests was the economy run? Was it better to have had efficient, alien rule or that of local elites? Was British administration as free of corruption as it seems to have been? Was racism inevitably part of the British presence? Were the reforms of the twentieth century essentially self-serving or genuinely altruistic? Why, while they fought British imperialism, did Indians so passionately embrace English games such as cricket? If the English language and an effective railway system were benefits of British rule, were they worth it? Why did the British seek to 'civilize' a country whose basic culture was already 4,000 years old? Why did so many Indians apparently collaborate with the British, ape their social habits, and absorb their educational and political standards? If India was truly 'the jewel in the Crown', why did many British people find the Raj offensive and sympathize with Indian nationalism? Did the British set out to 'divide and rule' from start to finish?

The essence of the controversy, the doubts, dilemmas, and contradictions, can be gauged by examining what both Indians and British felt about the Raj, both in fact and in fictional representations, especially during the half century of the Raj's decline and fall.

During these years the British in India mainly pursued their traditional tasks of highminded administration and profitable business. There were, however, growing doubts about the purpose of British rule, especially as Gandhi's mass movement made its impact. It was not only the British who expressed their doubts. Some educated Indians found themselves torn between their nationalist convictions and the veneer of British culture that they had absorbed:

> I was picked out of the garbage and taken to school—that was done by the detestable British . . . the Imperialistic

British, who bothered to take up a gutter-boy and give him life. Am I grateful? I need not be so very. The British have a passion for alteration. I was educated at the Slane Memorial Scottish School for Orphan Boys. They had my mind and my body for seven years, and for seven years I learned to keep my heart shut away in darkness and starvation.[1]

Many British observers were also conscious of this dilemma:

You take these boys to England. You train them in the ways of the West, the ideas of the West, and then you send them back again to the East, to rule over Eastern people, according to Eastern ideas, and you think all is well. I tell you . . . it's sheer lunacy. . . . You have to look at the man as he will be, the hybrid mixture of East and West. . . . You take these boys, you give them Oxford, a season in London. . . . You show them Paris. You give them opportunities of enjoyments, such as no other age, no other place affords—has ever afforded. You give them, for a short while, a life of colour, of swift crowding hours of pleasure, and then you send them back—to settle down in their native States, and obey the orders of the Resident. Do you think they will be content? Do you think they will have their hearts in their work, in their humdrum life, in their elaborate ceremonies? . . . In England he is treated as an equal. Here, in spite of his ceremonies, he is an inferior, and will and must be so. . . . Will he be content with a wife of his own people? He is already a stranger among his own folk. He will eat out his heart with bitterness and jealousy.[2]

The coldness that British people were often alleged to feel towards India, sometimes prompted equal bitterness:

We Hindus are hard political bargainers on the surface, but underneath we're eager to be friendly human beings. Mother India never fails to respond to strangers who touch her heart, holding a flame of love and understanding to her imagination. A few English men and women . . . will always be welcome here. The rest of you we only endure because we must. You've patronised and bossed us for two centuries.[3]

Even while reforms unfolded during the early twentieth century, it was possible to face ridicule among the British community by asking for greater social contact with Indians.

Perhaps this great gulf was maintained largely by the British women in India. E. M. Forster, in his wonderfully perceptive and liberal novel *A Passage to India*, paints a deft picture of the dilemma:

She [Miss Quested] became the centre of an amused group of ladies. One said, 'Wanting to see Indians! How new that sounds!' A third, more serious, said, 'Let me explain. Natives don't respect one any more after meeting one, you see. That occurs after so many meetings.' But the lady, entirely stupid and friendly, continued. 'What I mean is . . . I was a nurse in a Native State. One's only hope was to hold sternly aloof.' 'Even from one's patient?' 'Why, the kindest thing one can do to a native is to let him die,' said Mrs Callendar. 'How if he went to heaven?' asked Mrs Moore, with a gentle but crooked smile. 'He can go where he likes so long as he doesn't come near me. They give me the creeps.' 'As a matter of fact I have thought what you were saying about heaven, and that is why I am against Missionaries,' said the lady who had been a nurse. 'I am all for Chaplains, but all against Missionaries.'[4]

Indians were often seen as wayward children needing firm handling:

> Stacy Burlestone was by nature essentially and fundamentally a kindly man; but long residence in the East and a wide experience of Orientals had led him to the conclusion, right or wrong, that, to the Eastern mind, kindness and weakness are synonymous. . . . He knew that the Indians' mental attitude towards the kindly and easy European is inevitably tinged with contempt; and that his translation of 'kind' is a word indistinguishable from 'soft'.[5]

Indian troops were frequently portrayed as being childishly dependent upon the adult qualities of their British officers, who were even able to deal masterfully with the fears unleashed by a cholera epidemic:

> Towards dawn the men came to us, a great company of them, though as you knowest, sahib, it is against the Queen's Regulations for sepoys to come to their officers in crowds, but see thou!—these were no longer soldiers: they were little children lost at night in the great bazaar, and crying for their parents. And they stood before Pollok Sahib and wailed and made obeisance and cried out together—'Send for the Colonel Sahib! He will take this torment from us. He will not let this thing be. It will not pass till he returns. But when he comes it will fly away for fear because of his great anger when he sees the evil it has wrought his children.'[6]

There were several ways of seeing the public schoolboys who, by and large, manned the Indian administration, or the Sandhurst cadets who officered the army. One version portrays them as a self-confident, rather casual, breed: 'the much-abused public school product in excelsis. No parade of brains or force; revelling in understatement; but they've got guts, those boys, and a fine sense of responsibility. . . . They're no thinkers, but they're born improvisers and administrators. They've just sauntered down the ages, impervious to darts of criticism or hate or jealousy.'[7]

The British were also seen as strong willed, old-fashioned patriots:

> Even in an age given over to the marketable commodity, England can still breed men of this quality. Not often in her cities, where individual aspiration and character are cramped, warped, deadened by the brute force of money, the complex mechanism of modern life, but in unconsidered corners of her Empire, in the vast spaces and comparative isolation, where old-fashioned patriotism takes the place of party politics, and where, alone, strong natures can grow up in their own way.
>
> It is to [those men] of an earlier day, that we are indebted for the sturdy loyalty of our Punjab and Frontier troops. India may have been won by the sword, but it has been held mainly by individual strength of purpose, capacity for sympathy, and devotion to the interests of those we govern. When we fail in these, and not till then, will power pass out of our hands. . . . Perhaps only those who have had close dealings with the British officer in time of

action or emergency realise, to the full, the effective qualities hidden under a careless or conventional exterior—the vital force, the pluck, endurance, and irrepressible spirit of enterprise, which it has been aptly said, make him, at his best, the most romantic figure of our modern time.[8]

The novelist and essayist George Orwell, who served for a time in the Burma police, gave another and much less flattering version of the servants of the Raj. He portrayed the British officer who

> had come out to India in a British cavalry regiment, and exchanged into the Indian Army because it was cheaper and left him greater freedom for polo. After two years his debts were so enormous that he entered the Burma Military Police, in which it was notoriously possible to save money. However, he detested Burma—it is no country for a horseman—and he had already applied to go back to his regiment. . . . He knew the society of those small Burma stations—a nasty, poodle-faking, horseless riffraff. He despised them.
>
> They were not the only people whom [he] despised, however. His various contempts would take a long time to catalogue in detail. He despised the entire non-military population of India, a few famous polo players excepted. He despised the entire Army as well, except the cavalry. He despised all Indian regiments, infantry and cavalry alike. It was true that he himself belonged to a native regiment, but that was only for his own convenience. He took no interest in Indians, and his Urdu consisted mainly of swear-words, with all the verbs in the third person singular.[9]

Edward Thompson, in *An Indian Day*, described the civil administration equally sharply:

> But intellectually the community was third-rate, and its mind was fed on starch and sawdust. . . . Administering the myriads evenly and firmly—administering them with an utter lack of perception of what was in the minds of a subject populace and with an unshakable conviction that he was in the place of God and could not err—if you like, doing his magnificent work like a damned fool—but has the world ever seen such glorious damned fools?[10]

Orwell believed that many British in India hated the worst aspects of the Raj:

> All over India there are Englishmen who secretly loathe the system of which they are part; and just occasionally, when they are quite certain of being in the right company, their hidden bitterness overflows. I remember a night I spent on the train with a man in the Educational Service, a stranger to myself whose name I never discovered. It was too hot to sleep and we spent the night in talking. Half an hour's cautious questioning decided each of us that the other was 'safe'; and then for hours, while the train jolted slowly through the pitch-black night, sitting up in our bunks with bottles of beer handy, we damned the British Empire—damned it from the inside, intelligently and intimately. It did us both good. But we had been speaking forbidden things, and in the haggard morning light, when the train crawled into Mandalay, we parted as guiltily as any adulterous couple.[11]

As the Raj drew to its end, it was tempting to see the relationship between Britain and India as one swinging between love and hate. E. M. Forster, as early as 1924, saw that a proper dialogue between Briton and Indian could not take place while one was the ruler and the other the ruled.

At the end of *A Passage to India*, Fielding, the British liberal, and the Indian, Aziz, ride together, and wrangle about politics. Aziz cried:

> 'Down with the English anyhow. That's certain. Clear out, you fellows, double quick. . . . We shall drive every blasted Englishman into the sea, and then'—he rode against him furiously—'and then,' he concluded, half kissing him, 'you and I shall be friends.' 'Why can't we be friends now?' said the other holding him affectionately. 'It's what I want. It's what you want.' But the horses didn't want it—they swerved apart; the earth didn't want it, sending up rocks through which riders must pass single file; the temples, the tank, the jail, the palace, the birds, the carrion, the Guest House, that came into view as they issued from the gap and saw Mau beneath: they didn't want it, they said in their hundred voices, 'No, not yet,' and the sky said, 'No, not here'.[12]

William Buchan, son of the novelist John Buchan, summed up Britain's contact with India in similar terms of love and hate. What he wrote in *Kumari* could serve as an epitaph for the British Raj:

> The whole thing is and always has been a love affair. First and last that's been what mattered. And it's taken the course, worse luck, of most love affairs, beginning with persuasion—none too gentle in this case—followed by delighted discovery, mutual esteem, ravishing plans for the

future, the first really frightful row, and a long, miserable cooling off into polite bickering punctuated by sharp quarrels and joyless infidelities, each side withdrawing, steadily and continually, more and more of its real self.

The first great quarrel, the only one that mattered, was the Mutiny—that wound went deep and we've never ceased to suffer, in a way. By then we'd let our character change for the worse. We'd stopped wooing excitingly, violently, with real strength and a lot of poetry. We'd grown a great big, bland evangelical face and were going about doing and saying things to people—God forgive us—for their own good.[13]

Perhaps all that can be said with any certainty is that Britain and the three constituent countries of the former Indian Empire—India, Pakistan, and Bangladesh—have a 'special relationship', a connection that is complex, affectionate, confused, and significant. The British were in India for 350 years, though not at first as conquerors and rulers. Nonetheless, this is a period far longer than almost any other imperial link—save that with Newfoundland, the eastern part of mainland Canada, and some Caribbean islands. The subcontinent has been indelibly marked by the long British presence, just as Britain's history has been undoubtedly changed by the lengthy association with India. Whether all of this has been for better or worse is almost impossible to say. But the interaction did happen and over an extraordinary number of years. Maybe it is sufficient simply to note and to celebrate that fact.

Chronology

883	King Alfred the Great sends Sighelm on a pilgrimage to India.
1498	Vasco da Gama reaches the spice port of Calicut on the south-west coast of India.
1556	Accession of Mughal Emperor Akbar; dies 1605.
1579	Father Thomas Stevens travels to Goa in India.
1583	Voyage of the merchant ship *Tyger* to Tripoli to send an overland expedition to India.
1600	Queen Elizabeth I grants a charter to the new East India Company.
1601	First East India Company ship sails to Sumatra to open spice trade.
1605	Reign of Mughal Emperor Jahangir begins.
1608	William Hawkins leads an expedition to Surat on the west Indian coast.
1615	Mission of Sir Thomas Roe to the Court of the Great Mughal at Agra.
1623	Massacre of Amboyna: the Dutch force the British out of the East Indies.
1627	Death of the Mughal Emperor Jahangir. Succeeded by Shah Jahan.
1641	Francis Day founds the base at St George, Madras.

1658	Shah Jahan deposed by Emperor Aurangzeb.
1661	Catherine of Braganza brings Bombay as her dowry to Charles II.
1690	Foundation of Fort St William, Calcutta.
1698	William III charters the New East India Company.
1707	Death of the Mughal Emperor Aurangzeb brings an increase in anarchy.
1708	The Old and New East India Companies merge as the United Company.
1757	Robert Clive asserts British supremacy in Bengal at the Battle of Plassey.
1772	Warren Hastings becomes Governor of Bengal.
1773	Warren Hastings becomes Governor General of British India. Parliament passes the Regulatory Act.
1784	William Pitt's India Act sets up Indian Board of Control.
1785	Hastings returns to Britain to face various charges.
1788	Impeachment of Warren Hastings on charges of corruption.
1795	Warren Hastings acquitted, but ruined.
1818	End of Maratha Wars.
1824-6	First Burma War.
1829	Suttee (sati—widow burning) abolished in Bengal.
1835	Macaulay's minute on education.
1839-42	First Afghan War.
1843	British conquest of Sind.

1845–6	First Sikh War.
1848–9	Second Sikh War; British annex the Punjab.
1852	Second Burma War brings whole country under British rule.
1853	British annex Nagpur.
1856	British annex Avadh (Oudh).
1857–8	Indian rebellion, or Mutiny.
1858	British government assumes sole rule of India; the Governor General is renamed the Viceroy.
1861	Indian Civil Service established.
1877	Queen Victoria proclaimed Empress of India.
1885	Creation of the Indian National Congress.
1898–1905	Lord Curzon is Viceroy of India.
1901	Death of Queen Victoria.
1905	Controversial partition of Bengal.
1906	Formation of Muslim League.
1908–9	Morley–Minto Reforms give Indians some significant representation in provincial and central government.
1911	George V crowned King-Emperor at Delhi Durbar. Capital moved to New Delhi.
1914–18	First World War.
1917	Montagu Declaration promises Indians 'responsible government'.
1918–19	Montagu–Chelmsford Reforms lead to the passing of the India Act of the same year, increasing Indian political power especially in provinces.

1919   First all-India *satyagraha* campaign led by Gandhi.
         Massacre at Amritsar. Government of India Act
         introduces dyarchy (joint rule) in provincial and
         central government.

1930   Gandhi leads salt march at Dandi.

1931   Irwin Declaration promises Indians Dominion
         self-government.

1935   Government of India Act, following Gandhi's civil
         disobedience campaign and Round Table talks,
         gives home rule to the Indian provinces.

1939–45 Second World War. Japanese conquer Burma.

1942   Bose forms Indian National Army, with Japanese
         help, to fight the Raj. Cripps Mission to solve
         constitutional deadlock ends in failure. 'Quit India'
         resolution leads to arrest of most of Congress
         leadership.

1946   Calcutta communal massacres. Indian Navy
         mutinies. Cabinet Mission to India

1947   Lord Mountbatten of Burma becomes the last
         Viceroy of India; the Indian Empire is divided into
         two separate states; India and Pakistan become
         independent, though members of the
         Commonwealth; Burma leaves the Commonwealth
         after independence.

1948   Gandhi assassinated by Hindu fundamentalists.

1949   India becomes a republic, though choosing to
         remain in the Commonwealth. An important
         precedent is set for Commonwealth evolution, and
         the British monarch is henceforth known as 'Head
         of the Commonwealth'.

Sources for Quotations

Chapter 1. 'To fly to India for gold': Early Contacts, 1583–1615

1. *Anglo-Saxon Chronicle*, ed. and trans. B. Thorpe (1861), i. 150 and ii. 66; quoted in H. G. Rawlinson, *British Beginnings in Western India 1579–1657* (Oxford: Clarendon Press, 1920), 21.

2. D. Macpherson, *Annals of Commerce* (1805 edn.), ii. 39, quoted in Rawlinson, *Beginnings in Western India*, 22.

3. R. Sencourt, *India in English Literature* (London: Simpkin Marshall, 1924), 62, footnotes C. Marlowe, *1 Tam.* I. I.

4. Ibid. 67, credits C. Marlowe, *Faustus*, I. I.

5. Ibid. 127, notes 'Milton in *Paradise Lost* wrote this'.

6. Rawlinson, *British Beginnings in Western India*, 27.

7. Sencourt, *India in English Literature*, 65.

8. Brian Gardner, *The East India Company: A History* (London: Hart-Davis, 1971), 23.

9. Ibid. 26.

10. Ibid. 30.

11. Ibid. 32.

Chapter 2. 'Infamous for their honest endeavours': Laying Foundations, 1615–1708

1. W. Foster (ed.), *The Embassy of Sir Thomas Roe* (London: Humphrey Milford, 1926), 71.

2. Letter from Sir Thomas Roe to the East India Company, dated 24 November 1616, in ibid. 310.

3. Ibid.

4. Brian Gardner, *The East India Company: A History* (London: Hart-Davis, 1971), 50.

5. C. Fawcett, *The English Factories in India: The Western Presidency 1670–1677* (Oxford: Clarendon Press, 1936), 19, footnoted as 'Bombay Let. 3 Nov., 1670, 105 Sur. 55 and O.C. 3509.

6. Gardner, *The East India Company*, 41.

7. Henry Martyn, *The Advantages of the East-India Trade to England Consider'd* (London: J. Roberts, 1720), 2.

8. Sir Jadunath Sarkar, *Shivaji and his Times* (Delhi: Orient Longman, 1973), 208.

9. General letter to Fort St George, dated London, 28 September 1687 (subtitled Public Despatches from England, viii. 181–204), in *Records of Fort St George: Despatches from England 1686–92*, viii (Madras: Government Press, 1926), 83.

10. H. Yule (ed.), *The Diary of William Hedges, Esq.: during his Agency in Bengal . . . 1681–1687*, 3 vols. (London: Hakluyt Society, 1888) ii. 46; contained in correspondence from Job Charnock to Hugli Council, dated 6 July 1678.

11. R. Hudson (ed.), *The Raj: An Eyewitness Account of the British in India* (London: Folio Society, 1999), 24–5.

Chapter 3. Conquest and Corruption: The Struggle for Supremacy, 1708–1815

1. Percival Spear, *The Oxford History of Modern India 1740–1975* (2nd edn.; Delhi: Oxford University Press, 1978), 22.

2. J. Law (Law de Lauriston), 'Mémoire sur quelques affaires de L'Empire Mogol . . . 1756 à 1761', British Library, Eur. MSS (Orme) 272.

3.   Brian Gardner, *The East India Company: A History* (London: Hart-Davis, 1971), 153.

4.   Ibid. 114.

5.   Ibid. 123.

6.   Ibid. 97.

7.   W. W. Hunter, *Annals of Rural Bengal* (London: Smith & Elder, 1897), 26.

8.   L. S. S. O'Malley, *History of Bengal, Bihar and Orissa under British Rule* (Calcutta: Bengal Secretariat, 1925), 359.

9.   C. Grant, 'Observations in the State of Society among the Asiatic Subjects of Great Britain', particularly with respect to Morals . . . Written Chiefly in the Year 1792, British Library, Eur. MSS., E93, fo. 81ᵛ.

10. James Mill, *History of British India* (abridged edn.; Chicago: University of Chicago, 1975), 556.

11. Gardner, *The East India Company*, 77.

12. Ibid. 139.

13. Ibid. 127.

14. Letter dated London, 3 January 1710, para. 99, in *Records of Fort St George: Despatches from England 1706–10*, xv (Madras: Government Press, 1927), 146.

15. General letter to Fort Marlborough, dated London, 14 March 1717, in *Records of Fort St George: Despatches from England 1710–21*, xvi–xxiii (Madras: Government Press, 1927), 32.

16. General Letter to Fort St George, dated London, 26 April 1721, in ibid. 99.

17. Dispatch to Bengal, dated London, 12 January 1714, paras. 61, 80, in East India Company Records: Correspondence with India, Letter Book 15.

18. Dispatch to St Helena, dated London, 22 February 1716, para. 69, in East India Company Records: Correspondence with India, Letter Book 16.

Chapter 4. 'The great ends we have in view': The East India Company as Paramount Power, 1815–1857

1. Rudyard Kipling, 'The Young British Soldier', in *Definitive Edition of Rudyard Kipling's Verse* (London: Hodder & Stoughton, 1949), 416.

2. Flora Annie Steel, *On the Face of the Waters* (London: Wm. Heinemann, 1897), 135.

3. J. Lang, *Wanderings in India* (London: Routledge, Warne & Routledge, 1859), 107.

4. Mrs Colin Mackenzie, *Life in the Mission, the Camp, and the Zenana*, 2 vols. (London: Richard Bentley, 1854), i. 278.

5. J. W. Kaye, *Peregrine Pulteney, or Life in India*, 3 vols. (London: John Mortimer, Adelaide Street, 1844), ii. 130.

6. Ibid. ii. 102.

7. Mrs Postans, *Western India in 1838*, 2 vols. (London: Saunders & Otley, 1839), i. 165.

8. J. C. Maitland, *Letters from Madras by a Lady* (London: John Murray, 1843), 40–2.

9. Ibid. 140.

10. J. H. Stocqueler, *Handbook to India* (London: Wm. H. Allen, 1845), 92.

11. W. H. Sleeman, *Rambles and Recollections of an Indian Official*, 2 vols. (Westminster: Archibald Constable, 1893), ii. 321.

12. Lady Emma Edwardes, *Memorials of the Life and Letters of Major-General Sir Herbert B. Edwardes*, 2 vols. (London: Kegan, Paul & Trench, 1886), i. 14.

13. Captain Bellow, *Memoirs of a Griffin, or a Cadet's First Year in India*, 2 vols. (London: Wm. H. Allen, 1843), i. 112.

14. Lord Frederick Roberts, *Forty-One Years in India: From Subaltern to Commander-in-Chief* (London: Richard Bentley, 1898), 3.

15. Maitland, *Letters from Madras by a Lady*, 53.

16. J. Malcolm, *The Political History of India from 1784 to 1832*, 2 vols. (London: John Murray, 1826), ii. 183–5.

17. G. M. Young (ed.), *Speeches by Lord Macaulay with his Minute on Indian Education* (London: Oxford University Press, 1935), 359.

18. B. B. Majumdar, *Indian Political Associations and Reform of Legislature (1818–1917)* (Calcutta: Firma K. L. Mukhopadhyay, 1965), 57.

19. J. Peggs, *India's Cries to British Humanity* (3rd edn.; London: Simpkin and Marshall, 1832), 224.

20. M. Edwardes, *British India 1772–1947* (London: Sidgwick & Jackson, 1967), 98.

21. Sleeman, *Rambles and Recollections of an Indian Official*, i. 178, 225.

Chapter 5. 'The devil's wind': The Great Indian Uprising, or Mutiny, of 1857–1858

1. James Lunt (ed.), *From Sepoy to Subedar: Being the Life and Adventures of Subedar Sita Ram, a Native Officer of the Bengal Army*, Written and Related by himself (London: Macmillan Papermac, 1988), 25.

2. Brian Gardner, *The East India Company: A History* (London: Hart-Davis, 1971), 271.

3. Katherine Bartrum, *A Widow's Reminiscences of the Siege of Lucknow* (London: James Nisbet, 1858), 22.

4. Ibid. 50.

5. Ibid. 52.

6. Gardner, *The East India Company*, 268.

7. Ibid. 283.

8. G. Trevelyan, *The Competition Wallah* (London: Macmillan, 1895), 251.

9. Ibid. 243.

Chapter 6. Lords of All they Surveyed? The Raj at its Zenith, 1858–1905

1. V. C. Prinsep, *Imperial India: An Artist's Journals* (London: Chapman & Hall, 1879), 32.

2. Ibid. 36.

3. Lady Betty Balfour, *The History of Lord Balfour's Indian Administration, 1876–80* (London: Longmans, Green, 1899), 119.

4. *Observations by Miss Nightingale . . . on the Sanitary State of the Army in India* (1862), 21 Nov. 1862, pp. 3, 6, 24.

5. M. Edwardes, *High Noon of Empire* (London: Eyre & Spottiswoode, 1965), 89.

6. Ibid. 92.

7. M. Edwardes, *British India 1772–1947* (London: Sidgwick & Jackson, 1967), 231.

8. W. W. Hunter, *A Life of the Earl of Mayo: Fourth Viceroy of India*, 2 vols. (London: Smith & Elder, 1875), ii. 321.

9. Ibid. ii. 320.

10. House of Commons Reports, 1904, vol. 63, paper 186, on the 'Moral and Material Progress and Condition of India during 1902–03', p. 173.

11. D. Judd, *Empire: The British Imperial Experience from 1765 to the Present* (London: HarperCollins, 1996), 264.

12. Edwardes, *High Noon of Empire*, 252.

13. J. Croker, *Diana Barrington: A Romance of Central India*, 3 vols. (London: Ward & Downey, 1888), i. 24.

14. Edwardes, *British India*, 182.

15. Ibid.

16. Hunter, *A Life of the Earl of Mayo*, ii. 303.

17. J. Strachey, *India* (London: Kegan Paul, Trench, 1888), 359.

18. British Library, Add. MSS. 49732, Curzon to Balfour, 31 March 1901, also quoted in Judd, *Empire,* 264.

19.   W. E. Gladstone, 'Aggression on Egypt and Freedom in the East', *Nineteenth Century* (1877); collected (London: National Press Agency, 1884), 10.

20.   *The Englishman* (6 March 1883).

21.   *The Englishman* (29 March 1883).

22.   Anon., 'The Poet's Mistake', *The Chutney Lyrics* (Madras; 1871), quoted in Edwardes, *British India*, 172.

23.   W. S. Blunt, *India under Ripon: A Private Diary* (London; T. Fisher Unwin, 1909), 264.

24.   Flora Annie Steel, *The Hosts of the Lord* (London: Macmillan, 1900) 71.

25.   'Pagett, M.P.', in *Definitive Edition of Kipling's Verse*, 26–7.

26.   V. D. Majendie, *Up among the Pandies, or A Year's Service in India* (London: Routledge, Warne, 1859), 267.

27.   P. Robinson, *In my Indian Garden*, 2nd edn. (London: Sampson Low, Marston, Searle & Rivington, 1878), 62.

28.   See also, Emily Eden's account of travel with her brother, the Governor General, in J. Dunbar, *Golden Interlude* (London: John Murray, 1955), 127.

29.   G. Trevelyan, *The Competition Wallah* (London: Macmillan, 1895), 113.

30.   'Route Marchin'', in *Definitive Edition of Kipling's Verse*, 426–7.

Chapter 7. The Beginning of the End? Reform and Conflict, 1905–1919

1.   D. Judd and P. Slinn, *The Evolution of the Modern Commonwealth, 1902–80* (London: Macmillan, 1982), 35.

2.   D. Judd, *Balfour and the British Empire* (London: Macmillan, 1968), 258.

3.   L. James, *Raj: The Making and Unmaking of British India* (London: Little, Brown, 1997), 451.

4.   Ibid. 458.

Chapter 8. Gandhi and the Fightback of Indian Nationalism, 1919–1939

1. D. Judd, *Empire: The British Imperial Experience from 1765 to the Present* (London: HarperCollins, 1996), 261.

2. *Madras Mail*, 23 April 1915.

3. *Indian Social Reformer* (1915).

4. D. Newman, *Harold Laski: A Political Biography* (London: Macmillan, 1993), 118.

5. Judd, *Empire*, 259.

6. M. Diver, *Far to Seek* (Boston: Houghton, Mifflin, 1921), 389–90.

7. L. James, *Raj: The Making and Unmaking of British India* (London: Little, Brown, 1997), 118.

8. *Allahabad Pioneer*, 5 May 1905.

9. Diver, *Far to Seek*, 394.

10. R. A. Butler, *The Art of the Possible* (London: Hamilton, 1971), 16.

11. D. Judd, *Lord Reading* (London: Weidenfeld & Nicolson, 1982), 218–20.

12. D. Judd (ed.), *A British Tale of Indian and Foreign Service: The Memoirs of Sir Ian Scott* (London: Radcliffe Press, 1999), 34–5.

13. E. Savi, *The Passionate Problem* (London: Hurst & Blackett, 1934), 36

14. M. J. Anand, *The Coolie* (London: Lawrence & Wishart, 1936), 30.

Chapter 9. 'Engine of War' or the Enemy Within? India, 1939–1945

1. D. Judd (ed.), *A British Tale of Indian and Foreign Service: The Memoirs of Sir Ian Scott* (London: Radcliffe Press, 1999), 112.

2. L. James, *Raj: The Making and Unmaking of British India* (London: Little, Brown, 1997), 542.

3. Ibid. 540.

4. 'Bloody Partition', Channel 4 TV, July 1997, producer Chris Mitchell.

Chapter 10. 'Tryst with Destiny': Freedom and Partition, 1945–1947

1. M. J. Akbar, *Nehru: The Making of India* (London: Viking, 1988), 366.

2. L. James, *Raj: The Making and Unmaking of British India* (London: Little, Brown, 1997), 595.

3. Ibid. 596.

4. Ibid. 597.

5. K. O. Morgan, *Labour in Power, 1945–1951* (Oxford: Oxford University Press, 1985), 224

6. P. Ziegler, *Mountbatten: The Official Biography* (London: Collins, 1984), 473–4.

7. Akbar, *Nehru*, 410.

8. S. Gopal, *Jawaharlal Nehru* (Oxford: Oxford University Press, 1989), 5.

9. Akbar, *Nehru*, 420–1.

10. Ibid. 433.

Epilogue

1. R. Godden, *Breakfast with the Nikolides* (London: Peter Davies, 1942), 36.

2. A. E. W. Mason, *The Broken Road* (London: Smith, Elder, 1907), 31.

3. D. G. Stoll, *The Dove Found No Rest* (London: Victor Gollancz, 1946), 205.

4.   E. M. Forster, *A Passage to India* (Harmondsworth: Penguin, 1963), 27.

5.   D. Judd, *The British Raj* (London: Wayland, 1972), 112.

6.   A. Ollivant, *Old For-Ever* (London: T. Nelson & Sons, 1927), 125.

7.   M. Diver, *The Singer Passes* (London & Edinburgh: W. Blackwood, 1934), 426.

8.   M. Diver, *The Great Amulet* (Edinburgh: W. Blackwood, 1909), 211.

9.   G. Orwell, *Burmese Days* (London: Victor Gollancz, 1935), 223.

10. E. Thompson, *An Indian Day* (London: A. A. Knopf, 1927), 207.

11. G. Orwell, *The Road to Wigan Pier* (London: Victor Gollancz, 1937), 177.

12. Forster, *A Passage to India*, 316–17.

3.   W. Buchan, *Kumari* (London: Gerald Duckworth, 1955), 86.

Bibliography

Akbar, M. J., *Nehru: The Making of India* (London: Viking, 1988).

Allen, C. (ed.), *Plain Tales from the Raj* (London: André Deutsch, 1975).

Ashton, S. R., *British Policy towards the Indian States, 1905–1939* (London: Curzon, 1982).

—— *The British in India: From Trade to Empire* (London: Batsford, 1987).

Ballhatchet, K., *Race, Sex and Class under the Raj, 1793–1905* (London: Weidenfeld & Nicolson, 1980).

Basham, A. L., *A Cultural History of India* (Oxford: Clarendon Press, 1975).

—— *The Wonder that was India* (paperback edn.; London: Sidgwick & Jackson, 1988).

Bayly, C. A., *Indian Society and the Making of the British Empire* (The New Cambridge History of India, II.1; Cambridge: Cambridge University Press, 1988).

—— (ed.), *The Raj: India and the British, 1600–1947* (London: National Portrait Gallery Publications, 1990).

Belliappa, K. C., *The Image of India in British Fiction* (Delhi: B. R. Publications, 1991).

Bence-Jones, M., *The Viceroys of India* (London: Constable, 1982).

Bhattyacharya, D., *A Concise History of the Indian Economy, 1750–1950* (New Delhi: Prentice Hall, 1979).

Brown, J. *Modern India* (Oxford: Oxford University Press, 1985).

Bose, M., *The Lost Hero: A Biography of Subhas Bose* (London: Quartet Books, 1982).

Buettner, E., *Empire Families: Britons and Late Imperial India* (Oxford: Oxford University Press, 2004).

Burra, R. (ed.), *Looking Back: Film India, 1896–1960* (New Delhi: Directorate of Film Festivals, 1981).

Burton, D., *The Raj at Table: A Culinary History of the British in India* (London: Faber, 1993).

Chada, Y., *Rediscovering Gandhi* (London: Century, 1997).

Chakravarty, S., *The Raj Syndrome: A Study in Imperial Perceptions* (Delhi: Chanakya Publications, 1989).

Chamberlain, M., *Britain and India* (Newton Abbot: David & Charles, 1974).

Chandra, B., *India's Struggle for Independence, 1857–1947* (Harmondsworth: Penguin, 1988).

Charlesworth, N., *British Rule and the Indian Economy, 1800–1914* (London: Macmillan, 1982).

Chatterjee, A., *Representations of India, 1740–1840* (London: Macmillan, 1998).

Chaudry, K. C., *The Role of Religion in Indian Politics, 1900–25* (Delhi: Prakasham, 1978).

Copland, I., *The British Raj and the Indian Princes: Paramountcy in Western India, 1857–1930* (London: Longman, 1982).

Cronin, R., *Imagining India* (London: Macmillan, 1989).

Dewey, C., *Anglo-Indian Attitudes: The Mind of the Indian Civil Service* (London: Hambledon, 1993).

Edwardes, M., *High Noon of Empire* (London: Eyre & Spottiswoode, 1965).

—— *British India 1772–1947* (London: Sidgwick & Jackson, 1967).

—— *The Sahibs and the Lotus: The British in India* (London: Constable, 1988).

Fabb, J., *The British Empire in Photographs: India* (London: Batsford, 1986).

Ferguson, N., *Empire: How Britain Made the Modern World* (London: Allen Lane, 2003).

Fisher, M. H., *A Clash of Cultures: Awadh, the British and the Mughals* (London: Sangam,1988).

Forbes, G., *Women in Modern India* (Cambridge: Cambridge University Press, 1987).

Forster, E. M., *A Passage to India* (Harmondsworth: Penguin, 1963 edn.).

French, P., *Liberty or Death; India's Journey to Independence and Division* (London, Flamingo, 1998).

Gandhi, M. K., *An Autobiography* (London: Penguin, 1982 edn.).

Gardner, B., *The East India Company: A History* (London: Hart-Davis, 1971).

Gill, A., *Ruling Passions: Sex, Race and Empire* (London: BBC Books, 1995).

Gilmour, D., *Curzon* (London: John Murray, 1994).

Goonetilleke, D. C. P., *Images of the Raj: South Asia in the Literature of Empire* (London: Macmillan, 1988).

Goradia, N., *Lord Curzon: Last of the British Moghuls* (Delhi: Oxford University Press, 1993).

Greenberger, A. J., *The British Image of India* (Oxford: Oxford University Press, 1969).

Grewal, J. S., *The Sikhs of the Punjab* (The New Cambridge History of India, II.3; Cambridge: Cambridge University Press, 1990).

Gunderia, Y. D., *In the Districts of the Raj* (Bombay: Longman Orient, 1992).

Hamid, H., *Muslim Separatism in India: A Brief Survey, 1858–1947* (Oxford: Oxford University Press, 1971).

Haq, M. U., *Muslim Politics in Modern India, 1857–1947* (Meerut: Prakashan, 1970).

Hardy, P., *The Muslims of British India* (Cambridge: Cambridge University Press, 1972).

Hiro, D., *The Untouchables of India* (London: Minority Rights Group, 1982).

Hudson, R. (ed.), *The Raj: An Eyewitness History of the British in India* (London: Folio Society, 1999).

Ingall, F., *The Last of the Bengal Lancers* (London: Leo Cooper, 1988).

James, L., *Raj: The Making and Unmaking of British India* (London: Little, Brown, 1997).

Jones, K. W., *Socio-Religious Reform Movements in British India* (The New Cambridge History of India, III.1; Cambridge: Cambridge University Press, 1989)

Jones, S., *Merchants of the Raj* (Basingstoke: Macmillan, 1992).

Judd, D., *Jawaharlal Nehru* (Cardiff: University of Wales Press, 1993).

—— *Empire: The British Imperial Experience, from 1765 to the Present* (London: Phoenix Press, 2001).

—— (ed.), *A British Tale of Indian and Foreign Service: The Memoirs of Sir Ian Scott* (London: Radcliffe Press, 1999).

Juergensmeyer, M. (ed.), *Imagining India: Essays in Indian History* (Delhi: Oxford University Press, 1989).

Keay, J., *The Honourable Company: A History of the English East India Company* (London: HarperCollins, 1993).

—— *India: A History* (London: HarperCollins, 2000).

Khilnani, S., *The Idea of India* (London: Hamish Hamilton, 1997).

Kincaid, D. (ed.), *British Social Life in India, 1606–1937* (London; Routledge & Kegan Paul, 1973).

King, P. (ed.), *A Viceroy's India: Leaves from Lord Curzon's Notebook* (London: Sidgwick & Jackson, 1984).

Kipling, R., *Definitive Edition of Kipling's Verse* (London: Hodder & Stoughton, 1949).

—— *The Jungle Book* (London: Macmillan, 1961 edn.).

—— *Plain Tales from the Hills* (London: Macmillan, 1964 edn.).

—— *Kim* (Oxford: Oxford University Press, 1987 edn.).

Kulke, H., and Rothermund, D., *A History of India* (London: Routledge, 1986).

Lawson, P., *The East India Company, 1600–1857* (London: Longman, 1993).

Low, D. A. (ed.), *Congress and the Raj* (London: Heinemann, 1978).

Lunt, J. (ed.), *From Sepoy to Subedar: Being the Life and Adventures of Subedar Sita Ram, a Native Officer of the Bengal Army, Written and Related by himself* (London: Macmillan Papermac, 1988).

Lycett, A., *Rudyard Kipling* (London: Phoenix Press, 2000).

Macmillan, M., *Women of the Raj* (London: Thames & Hudson, 1988).

Marshall, P. J., *Bengal: The British Bridgehead, Eastern India, 1740–1828* (The New Cambridge History of India, II.2; Cambridge: Cambridge University Press, 1989).

Masani, Z., *Indian Tales of the Raj* (London: BBC Books, 1987).

Mason, P., A *Matter of Honour: The Indian Army* (London: Macmillan, 1974).

—— *The Men who Ruled India* (London: Cape, 1985).

Metcalf, T., *Aftermath of Revolt, 1857–1870* (New Delhi: Manohar, 1990 edn.).

Misra, B. B., *The Bureaucracy in India: An Historical Analysis up to 1947* (Oxford: Oxford University Press, 1977).

Moon, P., *The British Conquest and Dominion of India* (London: Duckworth, 1989).

Moore, L., *Maharanis: The Lives and Times of Three Generations of Indian Princesses* (London: Viking, 2004).

Moore, R. J., *Liberalism and Indian Politics, 1872–1922* (London: Arnold, 1966).

Moore-Gilbert, B. J., *Kipling and 'Orientalism'* (London: Croom Helm, 1986).

Moorehouse, G., *India Britannica* (London: Harvill Press, 1983).

Morris, J., *Stones of Empire: The Buildings of British India* (paperback edn.; Harmondsworth: Penguin, 1994).

Nandy, A., *The Intimate Enemy* (Delhi: Oxford University Press, 1988).

Nehru, J., *An Autobiography* (London: Bodley Head, 1936).

—— *The Discovery of India* (London: Meridian Books, 1946).

Pandey, B. N., *The Break-up of British India* (London: Macmillan, 1969).

Pemble, J., *The Raj, the Indian Mutiny, and the Kingdom of Oudh, 1801–1859* (Hassocks: Harvester Press, 1977).

—— (ed.), *Miss Fane in India* (Gloucester: Alan Sutton, 1985).

Porter, B., *The Absent-Minded Imperialists: Empire, Society and Culture in Britain* (Oxford: Oxford University Press, 2004.

Rawlinson, H. G., *British Beginnings in Western India 1579–1657* (Oxford: Clarendon Press, 1920).

Ray, R., *Industrialisation in India: Growth and Conflict in the Private Corporate Sector, 1914–47* (Oxford: Oxford University Press, 1979).

Robb, P., *A History of India* (Basingstoke: Palgrave, 2002).

Robinson, F., *Separatism among Indian Muslims: The Politics of the United Province's Muslims, 1860–1923* (London: Cambridge University Press, 1974).

—— (ed.), *The Cambridge Encyclopaedia of India, Pakistan, Bangladesh, Sri Lanka, Nepal, Bhutan and the Maldives* (Cambridge: Cambridge University Press, 1989).

Rothermund, D., *An Economic History of India* (London: Croom Helm, 1988).

Royle, T., *The Last Days of the British Raj* (London: Michael Joseph, 1989).

Said, E., *Orientalism: Western Concepts of the Orient* (London: Penguin, 1991 edn.).

Sarkar, S., *Modern India, 1885–1947* (Basingstoke: Macmillan, 1989).

Seal, A., *The Emergence of Indian Nationalism: Later Nineteenth Century* (Cambridge: Cambridge University Press, 1968).

Sen, S. N., *Eighteen Fifty-Seven* (New Delhi: Government of India Publications, 1957).

Sencourt, R., *India in English Literature* (London: Simpkin Marshall, 1924).

Singhal, D. P., *A History of the Indian People* (London: Methuen, 1983).

Steel, F. A., *The Complete Indian Housekeeper and Cook* (London: Heinemann, 1904).

Stokes, E., *The Peasant Armed: The Indian Rebellion of 1857*, ed. C. A. Bayly (Oxford: Oxford University Press, 1986).

Tadgell, C., *The History of Architecture in India: From the Dawn of Civilization to the End of the Raj* (London: Architecture & Design Press, 1990).

Talbot, I., *The Punjab and the Raj, 1849–1947* (Delhi: Manohar Publications, 1988).

Tammita-Delgoda, S., *A Traveller's History of India* (London: Windrush Press/Phoenix Press, 2002 edn.).

Thomson, E., *The Making of the Indian Princes, 1886–1946* (London: Curzon Press, 1978).

Tomlinson, B. R., *The Economy of British India, 1860–1970* (The New Cambridge History of India, III.3; Cambridge: Cambridge University Press, 1993).

—— *The Political Economy of the Raj, 1914–1947* (London: Macmillan, 1979).

Visram, R., *Women in India and Pakistan: The Struggle for Independence from British Rule* (Cambridge: Cambridge University Press, 1992).

Viswanathan, G., *Marks of Conquest: Literary Study and British Rule in India* (London: Faber, 1989).

Wolpert, S., *A New History of India* (3rd edn.; Oxford: Oxford University Press, 1989).

—— *Nehru: Tryst with Destiny* (Oxford: Oxford University Press, 1996).

Woodford, P., *The Rise of the Raj* (Speldhurst: Midas Books, 1978).

Index